A Flavour of
Normandy

A Flavour of
Normandy

Carole Clements

Illustrations by Paul Collicutt

HEADLINE

A QUARTO BOOK

Copyright © 1996 Quarto Publishing plc
First published in Great Britain in 1996 by
HEADLINE BOOK PUBLISHING

HEADLINE BOOK PUBLISHING
A division of Hodder Headline PLC
338 Euston Road
London NW1 3BH

British Library Cataloguing in Publication Data

Clements, Carole
Flavour of Normandy
I. Title
641.5944

ISBN 0-7472-1636-3

SENIOR EDITOR Kate Kirby
DESIGNER Suzie Hooper, Lindsey Johns
ART EDITORS Anne Fisher, Liz Brown
TEXT EDITOR Deborah Savage
PICTURE RESEARCHER Susannah Jayes
ILLUSTRATOR Paul Collicutt
PICTURE RESEARCH MANAGER Giulia Hetherington
EDITORIAL DIRECTOR Mark Dartford
ART DIRECTOR Moira Clinch

Typeset in Great Britain by Central Southern Typesetters, Eastbourne
Manufactured in Hong Kong by Regent Publishing Services Ltd
Printed in China by Leefung-Asco Printers Ltd

The author wishes to express her appreciation to Jane Sigal, whose thorough, dependable and inspired
research into the people and products of Normandy was of enormous assistance. Anyone travelling to
this part of France – or hoping to – should have her superb book, *Normandy Gastronomique*.
Profound thanks also to Jessica Palmer for her invaluable assistance in recipe development and testing,
and for her patient and critical editorial eye.
Most sincere gratitude is due, also, to Tim Garland, whose affection and constant support not only
make this work possible, but infinitely more rewarding.

Contents

Flavourful, freshly churned farmhouse butter is often available on market stalls and in cheese shops and fine delicatessens.

Introduction

A lush, rolling patchwork of varying shades of green, contained by the sea, dissected by rivers and punctuated by orchards whose boughs reveal the progression of seasons, Normandy is particularly favoured by nature. Long one of France's richest regions, it is a land of ancient traditions finding its place in the modern world, with farming and fishing still at the very heart of its prosperity.

Sampling its food is the most pleasurable way of discovering Normandy. The local markets offer an array of farmhouse butter and cheeses, raw unpasteurized cream so thick you can hardly ladle it out, home-raised chickens, ducks and geese and fresh eggs. In season, you will find wild mushrooms gathered in local forests and young shallot shoots that look like spring onions. Fishermen's wives proffer the day's catch: Dover soles, skate, brill, mackerel, scallops, mussels, oysters and lobsters. There is abundant produce from large commercial farms, but also small *ad hoc* market stalls selling the overflow from a nearby farmer's own vegetable patch – bundles of slim leeks or chard, robust lettuces and cabbages. Markets thrive all over Normandy and wandering through the stalls, taking in the sounds and the scents, gives a real sense of local colour.

In Normandy, the pride of the artisan endures and competitions abound to determine the best black pudding, brioche, and *bourdalots* (apple pastries); the definitive trout pâté or wild-mushroom terrine. Fairs and festivals celebrate cherry-picking, cider-making and the advent of the scallop and herring seasons. Gastronomic societies flourish. Almost every town has one, from the *Vikings du Bocage*, who hold an annual sausage competition in the southern part of the Manche, to the *Confrérie Gastronomique Normande de la Tripière Fertoise*, who dress in flowing robes to award the yearly prize for the best *tripes en brochette*, the tripe parcels that are a speciality of La Ferté-Macé. Normans take the conservation of their culinary traditions seriously and they have a good time doing it.

THE TASTE OF NORMANDY

The products that signal Normandy – and these are not limited to cream and apples – are all characterized by a natural quality that comes from the wealth of the land and sea. The best food requires the finest ingredients, and the meals in Normandy are justly memorable.

Seafood of the finest quality is brought in daily by local fishermen to Normandy's many ports. The oyster and mussel beds in the English Channel are among the most productive anywhere, and carefully monitored fishing and harvesting promotes conservation of these essential marine resources. Fish and shellfish play an important role in the traditional – and contemporary – cuisine of the region.

Dairy products are superb. Milk, cream and butter are fundamental to Norman cooking and, until recently, cream was a common feature of almost every course. The rich cream and the tangy *crème fraîche* are so full of flavour that often just a little will suffice to transform a dish and impart an authentic Normandy flavour. The butter also has a refined taste and quality and is used extensively. But perhaps more than anything else, Normandy is famous for its cheese.

Cheese-making traditions go back more than 900 years. *Neufchâtel* was documented as early as 1035, and is still one of four Normandy cheeses recognized with an *Appellation d'Origine Contrôlé*. Often shortened to AOC, this serves as a kind of guarantee of regional authenticity and quality, specifying the area and methods of production. The other AOC cheeses are *Camembert, Livarot* and *Pont-l'Evêque*, but the list of fine Normandy cheeses doesn't stop there.

Most of Normandy's 750,000 cattle are raised for dairy products, but veal and beef are excellent here, as well as beef offal. Long-simmered tripe made in the traditional pottery casserole, *tripes à la mode de Caen*, has been a local speciality for generations. Pork is equally intrinsic to Norman cooking, providing *charcuterie* as well as fresh meat. Longstanding traditions of sausage-making and ham-curing

are still carried on: the famed *andouille* from Vire, black pudding from Mortagne-au-Perche, smoked ham from around Saint-Lô. Along with the old, new products, such as the *fois gras* now produced very successfully, are becoming part of regional Norman fare.

Apples, Cider and Calvados

The climate and soil composition in Normandy favour the cultivation of apples and they feature significantly in savoury dishes as well as sweet. Normandy excels in the production of alcoholic drinks made from apples – cider, Calvados and Pommeau – and these are used extensively in the cooking of the region.

A wide range of apple varieties is cultivated, many exclusively for cider production. An apple variety will develop different characteristics when grown in different kinds of soil, in much the same way as a wine acquires its individuality. This leads to a diversity of character in the ciders produced in different areas. Follow the "cider routes" of Normandy – the itineraries signposted in the cider-producing areas – and you will have the opportunity of tasting an extraordinary variety of ciders.

Calvados is a potent spirit distilled from cider. As early as 1553, references to *eau-de-vie de cidre*, or cider brandy, appeared in the diary of Gilles de Gouberville, a gentleman

The sweet-sour scent of cider apples awaiting pressing perfumes the autumn air.

farmer. The guild of apple-brandy distillers was formed during the seventeenth century, but it wasn't until the nineteenth century that the apple brandies made in this part of France acquired the name Calvados. In 1941, Calvados received AOC classification.

Pommeau, served as an *apéritif*, is a blend of the juice of fresh-pressed cider apples and Calvados, aged in wooden barrels. It is less readily available outside France than Calvados and must be made in the same AOC production area. Even more rare is the pear cider or perry, *poiré*, made in the area around Domfront in the Orne.

NORMANDY IN FIVE PARTS

Normandy is divided into five administrative *départements*, or counties, and each has its own character. In Seine-Maritime and Calvados, fishermen and farmers ply their separate occupations and only meet in the marketplace. In the Manche, these two primary lifestyles are more closely related, perhaps because, surrounded by water, the land is profoundly affected by it. The Orne is landlocked, so the focus is primarily agricultural; the Eure has a snip of coast but no ports, so, equally, it is agrarian in outlook.

The geographic divisions, used by the people themselves, do not always coincide with the departmental boundaries. They come more from the lie of the land, so the wide fertile chalk plateau inland from the ports of the Seine-Maritime is called the *Pays de Caux*, the land of chalk. The *Pays d'Auge*, one of the richest areas of cheese production and apple cultivation, continues down into the Orne from Calvados, and the *Bocage*, identified by high hedgerows, takes in parts of three *départements*.

SEINE-MARITIME

This is perhaps the most diverse of the five *départements*. The territory ranges from the Alabaster coast, captured by Monet, where fishing boats set out from numerous ports nestling in the chalk cliffs rising from the sea, to the lush fields of the *Pays de Caux*, the windswept plateau where grains and sugar beets thrive and orchards nourish cows as well as people, to the rolling meadows of the *Pays de Bray* with dairy herds everywhere you look. The harvest from land and sea is equally rich.

The chalk cliffs of Etretat are familiar to everyone who knows Monet's paintings.

Dieppe, the leading port of Renaissance France, still plays an active role in fishing today. Sole, plaice, turbot, brill and mackerel, among other fish, are landed here. Dieppe is said to provide about 40 per cent of the shellfish consumed in France and it is particularly famed for scallops. The Seine Bay has the most extensive and bountiful scallop bed in the English Channel.

Fécamp is Normandy's primary cod-fishing port, with cod-drying and herring-processing industries. It is also the home of *Bénédictine* liqueur, flavoured with 27 herbs and spices, invented in 1510 by a monk of the Benedictine order as a tonic. In the mid-nineteenth century, the formula was rediscovered quite by accident by a Norman businessman, Alexandre Legrand, who decided to re-launch it as a liqueur.

Every coastal village in Seine-Maritime seems to have a few fishing boats dotting its pebbled shores, attesting to the continuing importance of this way of life. Inland from the coast, the emphasis switches from fishing to farming.

The *Pays de Caux* is a primary area for the cultivation of wheat, corn, flax and the sugar beets that can be seen heaped in huge piles at the sides of the fields after harvest. Beetroot for the table is also grown, along with various berries. Orchards are prolific and, to maximize their use, they often double as grazing land for dairy cattle, who munch the occasional apple. The apple and cider route, *route de la pomme et du cidre*, linking the *Pays de Caux* with the *Pays de Bray*, is good for discovering the local drinks made in this part of Normandy.

Less intensively cultivated, the *Pays de Bray* in the northernmost inland part of Normandy, is called the "dairy of Paris". This gentle bit of bucolic countryside is a centre for cheese production, with the town of Neufchâtel as its "dairy capital". The *route du fromage de Neufchâtel* leads you along a circuit to sample the oldest of Normandy's cheeses.

In the Seine valley, the river that has long served as a natural supply route to Paris flows through Rouen, the largest city in Normandy. (Rouen cathedral attests to the gourmandizing of the city's medieval residents, with a tower funded by dispensations to allow the consumption of butter during Lent.) In this valley, the warm, humid air from the river brings the apple trees into blossom several weeks before those in the *Pays de Caux*. The prolific cultivation of apples, cherries and pears is evident along the *route des fruits* between Jumièges, with its magnificent ruined abbey, and Duclair, known for its succulent ducks.

CALVADOS

This is the *département* that most resembles archetypal Normandy – country villages with half-timbered houses, rich and peaceful countryside, orchards and lazy cows. The origin of its name is Spanish, taken from one of the ships of the Armada, *El Calvador*, which struck a reef off the Normandy coast. Bustling beaches and

This peaceful scene is typical in the Vallée d'Auge, known for its cream and apples.

picturesque ports line its 120-kilometre coast, a coast that has borne the brunt of battle more than once.

The stretch of coast between Honfleur and Cabourg is Normandy's most fashionable, with Deauville at its centre. The old harbour at Honfleur, once a gateway to the North American colonies, is still picture-perfect and local fishermen hawk their tiny brown shrimps, *crevettes grises* – so good with brown bread and sweet butter and a cider chaser – on the quay.

Inland, the verdant pastures and wooded valleys of the *Pays d'Auge* take in much of eastern Calvados. Exquisite villages, like Le Bec-Hellouin whose half-timbered houses look much as they did in the seventeenth and eighteenth centuries, and colourful patterned brick manor houses affirm the prosperity of this part of Normandy. The *Pays d'Auge* is cheese and apple country – *Camembert, Pont-l'Evêque* and *Livarot* are all made here, as well as a special double distilled Calvados, with a separate AOC to distinguish it from the rest, and some of the best cider. On the *route du cidre du cru de Camembert*, the oldest cider route in Normandy, 23 producers offer tastings of their ciders.

Along the coast in western Calvados, charming ports like Courseulles-sur-Mer, renowned for its oysters, and Port-en-Bessin, one of France's more important fishing ports, are interspersed with World War II landing sites. Around Isigny, butter and cream are especially fine: the butter one of only two in France to have AOC recognition; the crème fraîche unique in this seal of approval.

Further south, the *Bocage* area is identifiable by its raised hedgerows, effective barriers during the most recent invasion of Normandy. Here previously cultivated fields were transformed in the nineteenth century to meadows and pastures. Villers-Bocage, with its Wednesday-morning cattle market, is a centre for the beef industry; Vire is the capital of smoked pork chitterling sausage. The *Bocage* reaches down into the Orne and extends westward, pushing into the southern part of the Manche.

Manche

In the Cotentin peninsula, known as the Manche after the bay into which it protrudes, you are seldom too far from the sea to smell the salt. But it is not just the air that is salty. The land near the coast is washed by the tides, and this gives a special quality to the lambs that graze in the meadows by the water's edge and the vegetables grown in the sandy soil. The moderating influence of the sea means that crops can be planted earlier and mature sooner, making this part of Normandy a source of early produce. With more than twice as much coastline as any other *département*, fish and shellfish are naturally an essential feature of the cuisine and the commerce.

Oyster- and mussel-farming are thriving occupations. On the western coast of the Manche, around Blainville, briny-tasting oysters are fattened for four years in open seawater in oyster "parks", where low platforms hold them off the sea floor. Near Saint-Vaast-la-Hougue, a yachting centre, oysters are washed by clean currents 12 metres down, acquiring a nutty flavour. Almost 20 per cent of France's oysters come from this *département*.

Mussels are farmed in a similar fashion, on stakes. They are also dredged from natural beds. Collection of wild mussels is strictly regulated, as is the harvesting of scallops, although the times and seasons vary from place to place. The tiny queen scallops, *pétoncles*, are a Cotentin speciality, along with small lobsters, called *demoiselles de Cherbourg*. The variety is superb – crabs, succulent venus and carpet-shell clams, even ormers.

Meat also features on the Cotentin table. Mont-Saint-Michel is one of the main sources of *pré-salé* lamb, which acquires a special flavour from the salty grass the animals eat. These tide-washed grazing lands bordering the shore extend further up the western coast to Briqueville-sur-Mer. Wood-smoked ham is still a speciality of the Manche and western Calvados, but farmers are now less likely to smoke their own hams, taking them to smoke-houses instead. Pork sausages are traditional, too, and competitions like the one in Saint-Hilaire-de-Harcouët in June encourage quality.

Even though the soil is stony and less rich in the Manche than in many other parts of Normandy, leeks, cauliflowers and cabbage flourish. Early vegetables, especially potatoes, are premium quality, and salad leaves and chicory thrive. The carrots that grow in Créances in salty, sandy soil at the edge of the sea are like no others and have received AOC recognition.

Coutances, a rich creamy cheese made around the town from which it takes its name, is one of the newest Norman cheeses. Historically, the Manche was not a cheese-producing area, but now Camembert and others are made here. Baking, however, is part of local heritage and traditional breads – dark, crusty country loaves and butter-rich brioche – are still baked in wood-fired ovens near Saint-Vaast-la-Hougue.

The gastronomic itinerary, *route de la table*, highlights producers of various artisanal products, but one of the most unusual spots is Villedieu-les-Poêles, a metal-working centre for more than 800 years. Copper pots in every conceivable size and shape fill the shop windows. The route wanders through the fruit-growing areas of the southern Manche that border the Orne.

ORNE

The Orne is the only *département* with no sea coast. Nonetheless, the landscape is greatly varied: stud farms and châteaux, market towns that come to life once a week and then settle back into their quiet rhythm, stone farmhouses adjoining orchards where cows rest under the trees and goats nibble the apples. Here you find traditional country life. Clods of earth left by passing farm machinery on wandering lanes reveal the rural nature of this part of Normandy and most of the farmhouses are occupied by farmers, not holidaymakers.

The terrain changes from one corner of the *département* to another. The *Bocage*, which continues into the Manche on the west and reaches north into Calvados, is an area of small farms lost in a patchwork of hedgerows. *La route de la poire* is a signposted circuit which explores the area around Domfront, home of pear cider (perry) or *poiré*. It includes manor houses as well as orchards and cider-producers. Both apples and pears are grown around here and you can distinguish the shape of the rounder apple trees from the taller, more pointed pear trees. The local Calvados is often distilled from a mixture of pear and apple cider.

The Orne is dotted with forests full of natural life. In the Andaines forest, *cèpes* are more plentiful than in Périgord. Further east, in Longny-au-Perche, an annual wild-mushroom terrine contest celebrates fungi collected in nearby woods. Wild deer roam the forests around Argentan, while in the rolling meadows, venison farming has opened a new area of commerce. At Haras du Pin, the national stud farm built in the seventeenth century by the architect who redesigned Versailles, horses live in greater luxury than some of the nearby farmers.

The *Pays d'Auge* embraces northern Orne, where

Cool, humid conditions are essential for proper ripening of Camembert cheeses.

Vimoutiers, a centre for Camembert production, and the tiny village of Camembert are found. The cheese museum in Vimoutiers houses a collection of artifacts and explains the cheese-making process. AOC Camembert is made in specified locations in Normandy, according to strictly regulated procedures. The curd, made from unpasteurized milk, is not cut or stamped, as is Neufchâtel, but ladled into the moulds in five *louches*, or ladlefuls. This ensures that the butterfat at the top of the curd is evenly distributed in the finished cheeses. The moulded curds are left to drain and the next day sprayed with a natural mould to stimulate the downy bloom which becomes the characteristic white rind. During the 20-day maturation period, the cheeses are turned several times and kept in cool, humid cellars. The *route du Camembert* leads you on a pilgrimage of producers. The Camembert cheeses that meet the AOC requirements are made in dairies, although often by hand; the two farmhouse cheeses made in Camembert itself do not have the government seal of approval.

Parts of this *département*, and indeed many other spots in Normandy, seem relatively untouched by the tide of modern life. People cling to the old ways and preserve the traditions of good food. Gastronomic orders help to instill pride in local culinary specialities; they improve the level of quality with competitions and fairs, such as the brioche contest in Moulins-la-Marche, the *bourdalot* and apple charlotte competitions in Athis-de-l'Orne and the *poiré* festival held alternate years in Mantilly.

There are two tripe contests in the Orne, one in the prosperous market town of La Ferté-Macé, the other in Longny-au-Perche, on the border of the Eure, where they also judge wild-mushroom terrines, and Mortagne-au-Perche hosts an international black-pudding competition which attracts visitors from far and wide.

Les Andelys, on the banks of the Seine, has great charm.

EURE

Normandy's most wooded *département* is dissected by five major rivers, including the Seine and the Eure; the latter forms part of its southern border. With only a snip of coast, you won't find any picturesque fishing ports or beaches; in their stead are sinuous rivers, cathedral-like beech forests and golden wheat fields. Of course, the ubiquitous apples that are Normandy's hallmark are part of the scene, with cider production on the increase.

The Apple House in Sainte-Opportune-la-Mare is helping to preserve traditional varieties of apples, primarily cider apples, but others as well. Their orchard boasts at least 50 varieties. Most cider is blended from the juice of several kinds of apples, to benefit from their different characteristics.

In this *département*, rivers are much more important than the sea. The only breath of salt air comes at the mouth of the Seine and this tree-lined "highway to Paris" is still used for transport. The Seine also flows near Giverny, Monet's home, with its cheerful blue-and-white-tiled kitchen and sunny yellow dining room; its glorious gardens are immortalized on his canvasses. With over 600 kilometres (375 miles) of rivers and streams for fishing, freshwater fish is a focal point in the regional cuisine. The gastronomic society in Bernay even sponsors a trout-pâté contest.

In the centre of the Eure, sweeping grain fields and intensive dairy-farming make the landscape less intriguing than the undulating riverbanks, but they contribute to the prosperity of the region. One of the newest regional products is *foie gras*. In the Eure, it is made more from ducks than geese and the duck meat, especially the thick fleshy breast, or *magret*, is a highly marketable byproduct. At Le Neubourg, *foie gras* markets are held monthly from October until Christmas and France's largest agricultural fair, *comise agricole*, takes place just before Easter.

Regional cheeses range from *Pont-l'Evêque*, one of Normandy's oldest cheeses (made also in Calvados), to *Cormeillais*, created only twenty years ago. Cheese-making is big business here, with soft cheeses such as *Boursin* and *fromage blanc*, as well as artisanal goat's milk cheeses.

The Gourmet Tourist

Normandy is well organized for gastronomic tourism. The cheese route, *routes des fromages Normandes*, takes in all the *départements*, with smaller, more focused circuits in particular areas, such as around Neufchâtel in Seine-Maritime or in the *Pays d'Auge*. Cider routes traverse the region, with one in the southern Manche, another in the *Pays d'Auge* and yet another in Seine-Maritime between the *Pays de Caux* and *Pays de Bray*. Most of these "routes" were developed within the last 20 years or so, and they are well signposted, with plenty of information available at local tourist offices.

Virtually every town of any consequence has a market at least once a week and these *marchés* are a great way to get a sense of local life. Food shops are usually grouped around the marketplace and visiting the bakeries and pastry shops to sample local specialities is a must. *Charcuteries* and *traiteurs*, where pork products and prepared foods are sold, often feature regional dishes such as tripe that are too time-consuming to prepare at home, thus keeping alive traditions that

might otherwise be lost.

This book provides a window into the great larder that is Normandy. For those who have travelled there and those who yearn to, it is a celebration of regional ingredients and local lore. Authentic recipes, both classic and contemporary, demonstrate how exciting and appealing the food of Normandy can be.

Every day, fishing boats set out from the ports sheltered in inlets in the chalk cliffs of the Alabaster coast, to mine marine riches. They come back with Dover sole, turbot, skate, mackerel and, perhaps, monkfish. Those that scour the rock formations just offshore return with lobsters, crabs, small bass and sole. These fishermen sell their catch on the pier or to restaurateurs or wholesalers. Most of the fish you eat in Normandy is only a day out of the sea and the fresh taste confirms this.

Dieppe, Fécamp, Port-en-Bessin – some of France's most active ports are in Normandy, but countless smaller seaport villages provide a local source of fish and seafood. With something in the neighbourhood of 500 kilometres (300 miles) of coast in Normandy, you are never far from the sea – especially in the Manche, a centre for oyster and mussel farming.

Oysters are fattened in open seawater in oyster "parks", on table-like platforms which

small boats like these play an important role in commercial fishing.

Fish and Seafood

hold them off the sea floor. Cultivation takes about four years and the molluscs are moved regularly, to give them more space as they grow. Saint-Vaast-la-Hougue, near the north-eastern tip of this peninsula, is another oyster centre. Its oysters taste different from those that come from the Blainville-Coutainville-Gouville basin on the western coast. Courseulles-sur-Mer in Calvados is also renowned for oysters.

several varieties of oysters are usually available in fishmongers' shops.

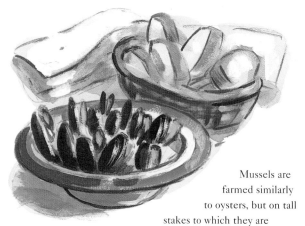

Mussels are generally cooked before serving, but oysters are most popular eaten raw, although some chefs explore other possibilities.

When you want to taste the fresh briny flavour of the sea, a shellfish platter, available almost anywhere on the Normandy coast, is one of the best ways to sample the local varieties. The seafood is served raw or simply boiled and chilled, and the selection is likely to include oysters, mussels, venus or carpet-shell clams, crabs, large or small prawns, cockles, winkles, sometimes raw baby scallops or perhaps ormers, which are collected during high tides. The tiered platter, set in the centre of the table, is served with shallot-infused vinegar, lemons and mayonnaise to dress the seafood, and accompanied by bread and butter.

Mussels are farmed similarly to oysters, but on tall stakes to which they are attached vertically in tubular nets. Wild mussels are also dredged from natural beds with metal nets. Mussels form the basis of many regional seafood recipes and the delicious liquid they yield during cooking provides wonderful flavour.

This seafood platter offers an opulent selection of local shellfish.

small lobsters, *demoiselles de Cherbourg*, often served poached in a *court bouillon* enriched with cream.

Normandy has more inland waterways than coastline; freshwater fishing, while more often recreational than commercial, is excellent. The rivers that cut through the *Pays de Caux* once provided power, but now they are more likely to produce trout. Trout-farming is carried on extensively here and in the Eure. In Bernay, which is surrounded by trout streams, the local gastronomic order puts on an annual contest, and the chefs of the town rise to the bait, with wonderfully decorated pâtés picturing anglers and their quarry on the top.

Fish, both freshwater and marine, and seafood of all sorts, are central to Norman cooking, and they are often combined with other regional products, especially cream, for memorable dining.

Scallops are found along much of Normandy's coast, and in Brittany, but the largest scallop bed in the Channel is in the Seine Bay off Dieppe, a major port since the sixteenth century. The scallops brought into Dieppe are large, plump and sweet. The season for scallop fishing is about seven months long, from early autumn through to late spring. Scallops are not migratory, so the reason behind seasonal regulation is primarily to prevent diminution of the population of this popular mollusc, but its flavour seems to suffer a little in hot weather. These regulations are strictly enforced; in many places the hours of collection are prescribed as well. An annual fair, held in Dieppe in November, the *foire aux harengs et à la coquille Saint-Jacques*, celebrates both the advent of the scallop season and the return of herrings to these waters.

Tiny queen scallops, called *pétoncles*, are dredged off the coast of the Manche. Another of the prized resources of the Cotentin peninsula is the

Marmite Dieppoise

NORMANDY SEAFOOD STEW

The tradition of exotic seasonings in Norman cooking goes back to the days of the spice trade with the Far East, when French ports were a gateway to northern Europe and Dieppe was a centre for ivory carving.

SERVES 8

1 kg (2 lb) live mussels, cleaned and de-bearded (see below)
Freshly ground pepper
5 tablespoons dry cider or white wine
15 g (½ oz) butter
1 garlic clove, very finely chopped
½ small fennel bulb, finely chopped
1 large onion, finely chopped
1 large leek, thinly sliced
1.5 litres (2½ pints) fish stock
1 kg (2 lb) firm-fleshed thick white fish fillets (Dover sole, turbot, cod, monkfish, etc.), skinned, if wished, and cut in pieces

500 g (1 lb) king prawns, peeled
500 g (1 lb) queen scallops, or sea scallops, quartered
1 teaspoon curry powder, or to taste
1 tablespoon cornflour
240 ml (8 fl oz) double or whipping cream
2 tomatoes, peeled, de-seeded and diced
Croûtons, to serve

Cook's Notes

Mussels need a little preparation, but they are worth the trouble. Under cold running water, scrape the mussel shells with a knife to remove any barnacles and pull out any stringy "beards". Discard any broken mussels and any open shells that refuse to close when tapped. Wild mussels, which are likely to be sandy, should be soaked in several changes of cold salted water. Cook mussels within an hour or so of cleaning them.

1 Put the mussels in a large, heavy pan with a little pepper and the cider or wine. Steam over high heat until the shells open (discard any that refuse to open). When cool enough to handle, remove the mussels from the shells. Strain and reserve the cooking liquid.

2 Heat the butter in a wide flameproof casserole or sauté pan over medium heat. Add the garlic, fennel, onion and leek and cook for about 3 minutes, until they start to soften. Add the fish stock and the mussel cooking liquid. Bring to a boil and then reduce the heat to medium.

3 Add the fish, starting with the thickest pieces and putting in the thinner ones after 2 or 3 minutes. A few minutes after all the fish has been added, put in the prawns, scallops and mussels and continue simmering gently for 2–3 minutes, until all the fish are cooked. Using a slotted spoon, transfer the fish and shellfish to a heated tureen and cover to keep warm.

4 Mix together the curry powder, cornflour and cream. Bring the soup to a boil and stir in the cream mixture. Continue boiling gently for 4–5 minutes, until slightly reduced and thickened. Stir in the tomatoes and taste for seasoning. Ladle the hot soup over the fish and shellfish and serve sprinkled with croûtons, if you wish.

Palourdes à la Persillade

CLAMS WITH GARLIC AND PARSLEY BUTTER

These clams are grilled with "snail" butter, which may sound more Burgundian than Norman, but you will find them in cafés and restaurants all over Normandy. The tasty garlic butter is also served on mussels prepared in the same way.

SERVES 4

48 medium clams
2 tablespoons water
100 g (3½ oz) butter
1–2 garlic cloves, finely
chopped

3 tablespoons chopped
fresh parsley

1 Under cold running water, scrub the clam shells with a brush. Discard any broken clams and any open shells. Soak in cold salted water for up to 30 minutes to remove any sand.

2 Put the clams in a large, heavy pot with the water, cover tightly, set over high heat and steam for 2–3 minutes until the shells open (discard any that refuse to open). When cool enough to handle, remove and discard the top shells. (If you wish, strain the flavourful cooking liquid through damp muslin and reserve or freeze it for another purpose.)

3 Beat the butter until soft, add the garlic and parsley and continue beating until well combined (use a food processor, if you wish).

4 Arrange the bottom shells containing the clams in a shallow baking dish on a bed of coarse salt or crumpled foil. Cover each with garlic butter.

5 Place under a grill or in the top of a preheated very hot oven until bubbly and browned, about 2 minutes.

Gratín de Coquillages

SHELLFISH GRATIN

This sort of gratin is typical throughout Normandy. You could substitute clams for the mussels, or use a combination, and add small scallops if you wish. It is very rich, but makes a delicious starter or light supper dish, served with a green salad.

SERVES 4–6

1 kg (2 lb) mussels, scrubbed and de-bearded (see page 20)	300 ml (½ pint) crème fraîche or double cream
2 tablespoons dry cider or white wine	3 eggs
30 g (1 oz) butter	360 g (12 oz) king prawns, peeled
30 g (1 oz) plain flour	3–4 tablespoons dry breadcrumbs
Freshly grated nutmeg	
Bay leaf	

1 Put the mussels in a large, heavy pot with the cider or wine. Cover tightly, set over high heat and steam for about 5 minutes until the shells open (discard any that refuse to open). When cool enough to handle, remove the mussels from the shells. Strain the cooking liquid through damp muslin and reserve 180 ml (6 fl oz) for the sauce. (Save the remainder for another purpose, frozen, if wished.)

2 Preheat the oven to 180°C/350°F/Gas Mark 4. Lightly butter a 28 cm (11-inch) gratin dish or 1.5 litre (2½-pint) shallow baking dish.

3 Melt the butter in a saucepan over medium heat. Stir in the flour and cook for 2 minutes. Add the reserved mussel cooking liquid and whisk vigorously until smooth, lifting the pan from the heat if the mixture starts to catch. Reduce the heat to low, add the nutmeg and bay leaf and stir in about half the cream. Continue simmering for about 5 minutes more. Remove the bay leaf.

4 Whisk the eggs and remaining cream together and slowly whisk in the sauce. Arrange the mussels and prawns in the dish and pour over the sauce mixture. Sprinkle with breadcrumbs and bake for about 50 minutes, until lightly browned on top, but still a little wobbly in the centre.

Moules au Cidre et à la Crème

MUSSELS STEAMED IN CIDER WITH CREAM

Not surprisingly, the excellent locally produced cider is used extensively for cooking in Normandy. It marries perfectly with the sweet, tender mussels farmed on tall stakes, or bouchots, *in beds off the Cotentin coast.*

SERVES 4

300 ml (½ pint) dry cider
4–6 large shallots,
finely chopped
Bouquet garni
Freshly ground pepper
2 kg (4½ lb) mussels, cleaned
and de-bearded (see page 20)

90 ml (3 fl oz) crème fraîche
or double cream
2 tablespoons chopped
fresh parsley

1 In a large, heavy pan, combine the cider, shallots, bouquet garni and plenty of pepper. Bring to the boil over medium-high heat and cook for 2 minutes.

2 Add the mussels, cover tightly and steam for 5 minutes, shaking and tossing the pan occasionally, until the shells open (discard any that refuse to open).

3 Remove the mussels to a bowl. Strain the cooking liquid through a sieve lined with muslin into a large saucepan and boil to reduce by half, about 7–10 minutes. Stir in the cream and parsley and add the mussels. Cook for about a minute more, to reheat the mussels.

superbly fresh seafood is widely available from market stalls, like these mussels on sale in Honfleur, one of Normandy's oldest ports.

Maquereaux au Cidre

MACKEREL POACHED IN CIDER

The best cider comes from the Auge valley, inland from the mouth of the Seine and the coastal fishing ports of eastern Calvados. This recipe is a good way to treat other fairly small fish, such as whiting, trout or sole fillets.

SERVES 4

2 mackerel, about 500 g
(1 lb) each, filleted
3 shallots, finely chopped
240 ml (8 fl oz) dry cider
Salt and pepper

180 ml (6 fl oz) crème fraîche
or double cream
Lemon juice (optional)
Chopped fresh parsley,
to garnish

1 Preheat the oven to 200°C/400°F/Gas Mark 6. Place the mackerel fillets in a lightly buttered, shallow baking dish. Sprinkle with the shallots and pour over the cider. Season with salt and pepper and cover tightly with foil. Bake for 15–20 minutes, until the fish is cooked through. Transfer the fish to a warm serving platter and cover to keep warm.

2 Pour the cooking liquid into a small saucepan and add the cream. Boil gently over medium heat for about 5 minutes. Season to taste, adding a few drops of lemon juice, if you wish.

3 Strain the sauce, pressing with the back of a spoon to extract all the liquid. Garnish the fish with parsley and serve with the cider sauce.

Silver-skinned, iridescent mackerel are brought in all along the northern coast of Normandy.

Coquilles Saint-Jacques à la Normande

SCALLOPS WITH MUSHROOMS IN CIDER CREAM SAUCE

Scallops from the Seine Bay, which has the most prolific scallop beds off the Normandy coast, are highly prized. There is even an annual festival in Dieppe to celebrate this rich, succulent mollusc.

SERVES 4 (OR 6 AS A STARTER)

300 ml (½ pint) dry cider
120 ml (4 fl oz) fish stock or water
2 shallots, finely chopped
Bay leaf
600 g (1¼ lb) sea scallops, rinsed
60 g (2 oz) butter
3 tablespoons plain flour
120 ml (4 fl oz) crème fraîche or double cream
Salt and white pepper
Freshly grated nutmeg
300 g (10 oz) mushrooms, sliced
Lemon juice
1 tablespoon chopped fresh parsley, to garnish

1 Combine the cider, stock or water, shallots and bay leaf in a saucepan. Bring to the boil, reduce the heat to medium-low and leave to simmer for 10 minutes. Add the scallops to the liquid, cover and leave to simmer for 3–4 minutes, until they are opaque. Remove the scallops with a slotted spoon.

2 Boil the cooking liquid until reduced to 240 ml (8 fl oz). Strain it and reserve. Pull off and discard the tough muscle on the side of the scallops.

3 Melt half the butter in a heavy saucepan over medium-high heat. Add the flour and cook, stirring, for 2 minutes. Add the reserved cooking liquid, whisking vigorously until smooth. Whisk in the cream and season with salt, pepper and nutmeg. Reduce the heat to low and leave to simmer for 10 minutes, stirring frequently.

4 Melt the remaining butter in a frying pan over medium-high heat. Add the mushrooms and cook, stirring frequently, until lightly browned and tender, about 5 minutes. Stir the mushrooms and scallops into the sauce and add lemon juice to taste. Transfer to a warm serving dish and garnish with parsley.

Goujonettes de Poisson à l'Estragon

SOLE AND SALMON WITH TARRAGON CREAM

Tarragon is a flavouring often found in Norman cooking, perhaps because it goes so well with cream. This simple preparation – combining superb Dover sole from the Channel and rich salmon – makes an elegant first course.

SERVES 4

360 g (12 oz) skinless
Dover sole fillets
360 g (12 oz) skinless
salmon fillets (the same
thickness as the soles)

Salt and pepper
360 ml (12 fl oz) double
cream
2 tablespoons chopped
fresh tarragon

1 Preheat the oven to 200°C/400°F/Gas Mark 6. Cut the fish fillets into long diagonal strips about 2 cm (¾ inch) wide. Season with salt and pepper.

2 In a heavy saucepan, heat the cream over medium-high heat. Add the tarragon and cook gently for 5 minutes.

3 Put the strips of fish in a shallow baking dish or individual ramekins and pour over the cream. Transfer to the oven and cook for 3–4 minutes, or until the flesh is opaque and set.

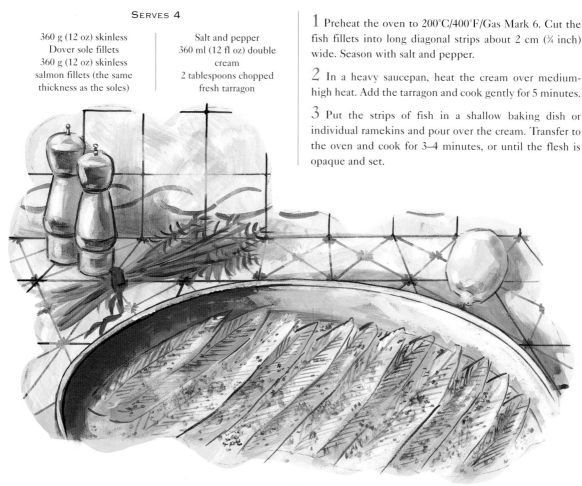

Sole à la Fécampoise

SOLE WITH PRAWN SAUCE

*Sole is prepared in many ways in Normandy. This recipe uses a prawn butter to
make the sauce – a style found in Fécamp, an important fishing port on the
Alabaster coast and the birthplace of the writer Maupassant.*

SERVES 4

500 g (1 lb) small or medium
cooked prawns in the shell,
with heads if possible
60 g (2 oz) butter
3 shallots, finely chopped
180 g (6 oz) mushrooms,
thinly sliced
240 ml (8 fl oz) fish stock

8 skinless sole fillets, about
150 g (5 oz) each
2 tablespoons plain flour
60 ml (2 fl oz) crème fraîche
or double cream
Salt and pepper
Lemon juice

1 Peel the prawns; reserve the shells.

2 Melt 15 g (½ oz) of the butter in a large saucepan over
medium heat. Add the shallots and cook for 2 minutes or
until just softened, stirring frequently. Add the
mushrooms and fish stock and bring just to the simmer.
Roll up the sole fillets and stand them in the pan. Cover
and poach until the flesh is opaque, for 5–7 minutes.
Remove the fillets to a warm dish and cover to keep
warm. Increase the heat and boil the cooking liquid until
reduced by one-third.

3 Melt the remaining butter in a heavy saucepan or
frying pan over medium heat and add the prawn shells.
Cook about 5 minutes, stirring frequently, until the
butter begins to colour and become aromatic. Strain the
butter into a clean saucepan, pressing firmly on the shells
with the back of a spoon.

4 Set the prawn butter over medium heat, add the flour
and cook for 1–2 minutes, stirring constantly. Gradually
whisk in the fish cooking liquid and pour in any other
liquid that has drained from the fish. Bring to the boil,
stirring constantly. Reduce the heat to medium-low and
cook the sauce for 5–7 minutes, stirring frequently.

5 Whisk in the cream and season with salt, if needed,
pepper and lemon juice. Add the reserved prawns and
the sole fillets and cook for 2–3 minutes to heat through.

The displays in fish shops are often as appealing as the products.

Truite Meunière aux Noisettes

TROUT WITH HAZELNUTS

Normandy has a vast expanse of coastline, but its many rivers also contribute to the wealth of fish. This classic preparation gets a new regional twist, with local hazelnuts in place of the more usual almonds.

SERVES 2

2 trout, about 360 g (12 oz) each, cleaned	60 g (2 oz) butter
3–4 tablespoons plain flour	30 g (1 oz) flaked hazelnuts
Salt and pepper	2 tablespoons dry cider

1 Rinse the trout and pat dry. Combine the flour, salt and pepper in a shallow dish and coat the trout lightly. Tap off the excess and discard any remaining flour.

2 Melt half the butter in a large frying pan over medium heat. Add the trout and cook for 6–7 minutes per side, turning once, until the skin is well coloured and the flesh next to the bone is opaque (check with the tip of a knife). Remove the fish to warm plates or a serving platter and cover to keep warm.

3 Add the remaining butter to the pan and sauté the hazelnuts until lightly browned. Add the cider and boil for a minute or two, stirring constantly. Spoon over the fish.

This tranquil river is one of many in Normandy favoured by anglers in pursuit of trout.

28

Barbue à l'Oseille

BRILL WITH SORREL SAUCE

This simple sauce, a speciality found in many fine restaurants in Normandy, is essentially sorrel melted in cream. It lends an appealing piquancy to any sweet-fleshed fish. Try it with salmon or turbot, as well.

SERVES 4

1 kg (2 lb) brill fillets or escalopes
Salt and pepper
30 g (1 oz) butter
3 shallots, finely chopped

210 ml (7 fl oz) double or whipping cream
180 g (6 oz) small fresh sorrel leaves, stems removed, washed and blotted dry

1 Season the brill with salt and pepper.

2 In a saucepan, melt half the butter and sauté the shallots over medium heat, stirring frequently, until soft and transparent. Add the cream and cook until slightly thickened, about 5 minutes.

3 Meanwhile, melt the remaining butter in a heavy frying pan and sauté the brill for about 3 minutes per side, or until it is opaque next to the bone (check with the tip of a knife). Remove the fish and keep it warm, loosely covered with foil.

4 Add the sorrel to the creamy sauce. Cook, stirring constantly, until the sorrel has completely melted. Spoon the sorrel sauce over the fish and serve.

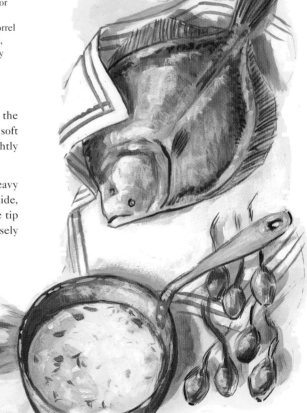

As you approach Mont-Saint-Michel, which seems to rise out of the sea, you are likely to see sheep near the water's edge. The lambs that graze in the salt marshes all along this coast of the Cotentin peninsula have a distinctive, salty flavour, which, combined with the leanness and tenderness of their flesh, makes them especially good, even roasted simply.

It is claimed that over one-quarter of France's meat and dairy products come from Normandy; while many of the cattle are raised for dairy purposes, veal and beef are excellent here, as well as beef offal. Tripe is a speciality in more than one area, sometimes simmered in a rich sauce, as is the preference in Caen, or

Meat, Poultry and Game

A typical Norman cow has dark brown spots and "spectacles".

rolled into parcels, as in La Ferté-Macé, the capital of *tripes en brochette*.

The *Bocage* area is a centre for the beef industry. Recognisable by its raised hedgerows, this area incorporates both the south-eastern part of the Manche and the south-western corner of Calvados, including Vire. The weekly cattle market on Wednesdays in Villers-Bocage starts at 6.30 am, with heavy trading in beef and dairy cattle. Further east in the Orne *département*, near its western border with the Eure, France's third largest weekly market gets

going at l'Aigle at about 7.30 am, with cattle traded informally rather than auctioned, while vegetable and other produce stalls are set up nearer the centre of the town.

Vire is known for *andouille*, the slowly smoked sausage made of pork stomach and intestines, cut in strips and arranged in concentric circles that are revealed when it is sliced. In Normandy, the pig is as important as the cow as a source of meat; the tradition of sausage-making embraces lean white pork, made into *boudin blanc*, pork blood for black pudding (*boudin noir*) and pork offal in various forms.

These longstanding regional traditions are carried on today by the *charcuteries* and *traiteurs*, shops for prepared food, as modern life makes preparing such things at home virtually impossible. Local contests and fairs both celebrate the heritage and uphold the standards of these regional specialities. The southern part of the Manche is a centre for curing and smoking country hams. Farmers used to smoke their own hams, but now local farmers bring them into smokehouses.

Tasty free-range farmhouse poultry is readily available in Normandy. The stalls in farmers' markets display chickens, poussins, ducks and geese. Brown hens and black-and-white speckled guinea fowl can be spotted in farmyards, foraging for food. Usually, the weekly market has a stall with rôtisseried chickens turning on spits, whose aroma makes it almost impossible to pass without stopping.

Spit-roasted chicken is a treat found in local markets and traiteurs.

Geese and ducks bred for foie gras provide Normandy's newest regional product.

often be seen hanging outside the shops. Much of the commercially available game – quail, rabbit and venison, which is being raised around Argentan in the centre of the Orne – is farmed. The meat is taken from young animals, so it is lean and mild in flavour, rather like beef.

Dovecotes, especially numerous in the *Pays de Caux* are a testament to the status of former manor house occupants. These were a symbol of privilege until the end of the eighteenth century, when the right of a lord to keep unlimited numbers of pigeons was abolished, since these birds would fatten themselves on the grain of nearby farmers. Now farmed pigeons are available from poulterers and butchers.

Normandy has a wide array of meat, poultry and game that more than equals the bounty it takes from the sea. Notwithstanding the wide availability of seafood, meat is an essential and beloved part of the Norman table.

A special breed of duck, canard de Duclair, raised in the Seine valley, produces a much higher proportion of breast meat and less fat overall than normal birds. It is thought to be a natural hybrid of domestic and wild ducks. Foie gras is now produced in Normandy from both ducks and geese, although ducks are more prevalent, and the region is becoming an important source of this delicacy.

French game laws, more liberal than in some countries, ensure general availability of wild game in season; game can

Filet de Porc Normande

PORK FILLET WITH APPLES AND CIDER CREAM SAUCE

The pork raised in Normandy is especially flavourful and this traditional recipe, combining it with apples and cream, is typical of the fare you might find in a gîte *or* ferme-auberge, *the farmhouse bed-and-breakfast accommodation in France.*

SERVES 4

2 pork fillets
Salt and pepper
45 g (1½ oz) butter
2 tablespoons Calvados
360 ml (12 fl oz) dry cider
120 ml (4 fl oz) chicken
stock or water
3 medium tart-sweet apples,
peeled, cored and
cut in eighths

2 shallots, finely chopped
180 g (6 oz) mushrooms,
sliced
2 tablespoons plain flour
120 ml (4 fl oz) crème fraîche
or double cream

1 Season the meat lightly with salt and pepper. Preheat the oven to 180°C/350°F/Gas Mark 4.

2 Melt one-third of the butter over medium-high heat in a heavy casserole just large enough to hold the fillets. Fry the meat, turning as needed, until golden all over. Add the Calvados, cider and stock or water. Bring to a boil, add the apple slices, cover and transfer to the oven. Cook for 20 minutes, or until the meat is cooked through. Transfer the meat and apple slices to a warm serving platter and cover them to keep warm. Strain the cooking liquid and remove any fat.

3 Melt the remaining butter in a medium saucepan over medium-high heat. Add the shallots and mushrooms and sauté for 4–5 minutes, stirring frequently, until they begin to colour. Sprinkle over the flour, stir to combine and cook for 1–2 minutes. Stir in the cooking liquid and simmer for about 5 minutes, until smooth. Stir in the cream and adjust the seasoning.

4 Slice the meat, coat it with a little sauce and serve the rest separately.

Farm products like cream are often sold direct from the producer.

Médaillons de Porc au Beurre de Noisettes

PORK STEAKS WITH HAZELNUT BUTTER

Hazelnuts are prolific in Normandy and in the autumn you find them fresh in the markets, still in their papery shells. For this recipe, the nuts should be toasted to heighten their flavour. To remove the skins, rub the nuts vigorously in a tea towel.

SERVES 4

75 g (2½ oz) hazelnuts, toasted and skinned	1 large pork fillet, about 500 g (1 lb)
75 g (2½ oz) cold butter	Salt and pepper
1 tablespoon chopped fresh chives	2–3 tablespoons Calvados

1 Put the hazelnuts in a food processor and pulse to chop them finely. Add 60 g (2 oz) of the butter, with the chives, and pulse until well blended but not pasty. Scrape the mixture on to a piece of cling film, shape it into a slim log, wrap and chill.

2 Slice the pork crossways into small steaks about 2 cm (¾ inch) thick. Season lightly with salt and pepper.

3 Melt the remaining butter in a heavy frying pan over medium-high heat. When it is foamy, add the meat and sauté it for 2–3 minutes per side or until just cooked through. Remove and keep warm.

4 Pour the Calvados into the pan, and boil briefly, scraping up any browned bits from the bottom of the pan. Pour it over the meat. Top each pork steak with hazelnut butter, dividing it evenly.

Navarin d'Agneau de Pré-salé

LAMB STEW WITH SPRING VEGETABLES

The lambs put out to graze by day in the salt marshes along the Normandy coast, often within sight of Mont-Saint-Michel, have a noticeable slightly salty flavour when cooked, for which they are highly prized.

SERVES 4

1 tablespoon vegetable oil
1 kg (2 lb) boneless lamb shoulder, trimmed and cut in 5 cm (2 inch) pieces
3 tablespoons plain flour
240 ml (8 fl oz) dry cider
360 ml (12 fl oz) lamb or chicken stock, or water
3 tomatoes, peeled, de-seeded and chopped
1 garlic clove, finely chopped
1 tablespoon each chopped fresh marjoram and thyme, or 1 teaspoon each dried marjoram and thyme

Salt and pepper
15 g (½ oz) butter
12–16 small shallots or pearl onions, peeled
360 g (12 oz) small new potatoes
360 g (12 oz) medium carrots, thickly sliced
150 g (5 oz) shelled peas (fresh or frozen)
2 tablespoons chopped fresh parsley

1 Heat the oil in a large flameproof casserole over medium-high heat. Add only enough lamb to fit easily in one layer and cook until well browned, turning to colour all sides. Remove the meat as it is browned and continue browning in batches. Return all the meat to the pan and sprinkle with flour. Cook for 1–2 minutes, stirring constantly. Add the cider to the pan and boil for 1 minute, stirring and scraping the bottom of the pan.

2 Stir in the stock or water, tomatoes, garlic and herbs and season with salt and pepper. Bring to the boil, skimming off any foam that rises to the surface. Reduce the heat to low and simmer, stirring occasionally, for 1½–1¾ hours, or until the meat is tender.

3 Meanwhile, melt the butter in a heavy saucepan over medium-high heat. Add the shallots or onions and season with salt and pepper. Cook, stirring frequently, until well coloured. Add 2 tablespoons of water, stirring and scraping the bottom of the pan; add to the casserole. (The recipe can be cooked ahead to this point; remove any fat and reheat gently before continuing.)

4 Cook the potatoes in boiling salted water to cover until just tender, about 15 minutes. Cook the carrots in the same way until just tender, about 10 minutes.

5 Remove any fat from the meat cooking liquid and stir in the potatoes, carrots and peas. Adjust the seasoning, if needed, and continue cooking for about 10 minutes more. Stir in the parsley just before serving.

The abbey of Mont-Saint-Michel, which seems to rise out of the sea at high tide, is surrounded by salt marshes where sheep graze.

Escalopes de Veau aux Champignons Sauvages

VEAL ESCALOPES WITH WILD MUSHROOMS

Hunting wild mushrooms is a favourite autumn pastime in the forests of Normandy. If you are unsure about any wild mushrooms you collect in France, you can take them to a pharmacy to be identified.

SERVES 4

360 g (12 oz) wild mushrooms (girolles, chanterelles, etc.)
90 g (3 oz) butter
1 garlic clove, minced

150 ml (¼ pint) double or whipping cream
500 g (1 lb) veal escalopes
Salt and pepper
3 tablespoons dry cider

Wild mushrooms are often seen on market stalls in the autumn.

1 Trim the mushroom stems and wipe the mushrooms with a damp cloth or, if necessary, rinse under cool running water and drain on paper towels.

2 Melt half the butter in a sauté pan or large saucepan over medium heat. Add the mushrooms, cover and cook for 2–3 minutes, until they produce some liquid. Add the garlic and continue cooking, uncovered, until the mushrooms are tender and the liquid has almost evaporated, about 10 minutes. Add the cream and simmer for 5 minutes more, stirring occasionally.

3 Season the veal lightly with salt and pepper. Melt about half of the remaining butter in a large, frying pan over medium-high heat. When the butter starts to brown, add the meat in one layer, cooking in batches and adding the remaining butter as needed. Cook for about 30 seconds on each side, turning the meat over when beads of juice appear on the surface. Remove the cooked meat to a warm platter and cover it to keep it warm. Add the cider to the frying pan and boil briefly, stirring and scraping the bottom of the pan. Stir the cider into the mushroom sauce and spoon the sauce over the meat.

Filet d'Agneau Normande à l'Estragon

LAMB FILLETS WITH TARRAGON SAUCE

Tarragon and cream are proven partners and this smooth sauce
complements the rich flavour of the lamb. It is elegant and very quickly made
– perfect for easy entertaining.

SERVES 4

750 g (1½ lb) boneless lamb
neck fillet, trimmed of fat
Salt and pepper
15 g (½ oz) butter
1 shallot, finely chopped

120 ml (4 fl oz) dry cider
180 ml (6 fl oz) crème fraîche
or double cream
1 tablespoon chopped
fresh tarragon

1 Season the lamb with salt and pepper. Melt the butter in a frying pan over medium-high heat and sauté the meat until well browned, turning once. Remove to a plate.

2 Add the shallot to the pan and cook for 1–2 minutes, until softened. Add the cider, bring to the boil, and reduce by half. Add the cream and tarragon, bring back to the boil, and reduce by one-third.

3 Return the lamb to the pan, with any juices. Taste the sauce and adjust the seasoning, if necessary. Simmer over low heat until the meat is heated through and done as preferred, about 5 minutes.

Poulet Valée d'Auge

CHICKEN WITH APPLES, CALVADOS AND CREAM

This dish, named for the Auge river that flows through northern Normandy,
features the apples and cider produced there. Many preparations use these
characteristic Norman ingredients and they are often similarly named.

SERVES 4

1.5 kg (3½ lb) chicken, cut
in 8 pieces
Salt and pepper
45 g (1½ oz) butter
240 g (8 oz) button
mushrooms
3 tablespoons plain flour
210 ml (7 fl oz) dry cider

360 ml (12 fl oz) chicken
stock
Bouquet garni
4 medium apples, peeled,
cored and quartered
3 tablespoons Calvados
120 ml (4 fl oz) double cream

1 Season the chicken pieces lightly with salt and pepper. Melt one-third of the butter in a large casserole over medium-high heat and brown the chicken, starting skin-side down and cooking in batches, if necessary. Remove the chicken when browned and pour off all but a tablespoon of the fat.

2 In the same pan, melt half the remaining butter and cook the mushrooms over medium heat, covered, until lightly browned, stirring frequently. Sprinkle on the flour and continue cooking for a minute. Stir in the cider and stock and bring to the boil. Return the chicken to the casserole, with the accumulated juices. Add the bouquet garni and bring back to the boil. Cover, reduce the heat to very low and leave to simmer gently for 25–30 minutes.

3 Meanwhile, in a non-stick frying pan, melt the remaining butter and sauté the apple slices over medium heat until golden. Pour over the Calvados and remove the pan from the heat.

4 Add the apples and Calvados to the casserole, with the cream. Simmer, uncovered, over medium heat for 5–10 minutes, stirring occasionally, until the sauce has thickened slightly and the chicken is cooked through.

Suprême de Volaille au Cresson

CHICKEN BREASTS WITH WATERCRESS SAUCE

*Vernon is best known because Giverney, Monet's home, is located in its environs.
The waterlilies immortalized by the French Impressionist painter are no more
prolific than the watercress that grows abundantly in the local streams.*

SERVES 4

4 skinless chicken breast
fillets, about
180 g (6 oz) each
Salt and pepper
2 shallots, finely chopped
120 ml (4 fl oz) dry
white wine
300–360 ml (10–12 fl oz)
chicken stock

Bouquet garni
180 ml (6 fl oz) crème fraîche
or double cream
2 teaspoons cornflour
120 g (4 oz) watercress
leaves, washed and
blotted dry
Watercress sprigs, to garnish

1 Season the chicken breasts lightly with salt and pepper.
Put the shallots in the bottom of a saucepan just large
enough to hold the chicken breasts in one layer and place
the chicken on top. Pour over the wine and stock, adding
a little more stock, if necessary, to cover; add the bouquet
garni. Bring the stock just to a simmer over medium heat
and poach the chicken breasts gently for about 10
minutes, or until the meat is springy when pressed.
Remove the chicken and cover it to keep it warm.

2 Remove any fat from the cooking liquid and boil over
medium-high heat until reduced by two-thirds. Discard
the bouquet garni.

3 Combine the cream, cornflour and watercress in a
blender or a food processor fitted with the steel blade and
purée until smooth. Add the cooking liquid and process
until the shallots are puréed.

4 Return the watercress cream to the saucepan, reduce
the heat to medium and boil the sauce gently for 2–3
minutes until it is slightly thickened. Adjust the
seasoning, if necessary. Return the chicken breasts to the
sauce and simmer for about 3 minutes, to reheat. Garnish
with watercress sprigs.

Monet's water garden is one of the artist's lovliest creations.

41

Lapin Braisée au Cidre

RABBIT BRAISED IN CIDER

In Normandy, rabbit is a popular meat and it is often cooked with the local cider. The mild, sweet flavour of rabbit resembles chicken, which may be substituted for it in many recipes.

Cider makers offer tours and tastings along the "cider route".

SERVES 4

1.2 kg (2½ lb) rabbit	1 carrot, finely chopped
Salt and pepper	360 ml (12 fl oz) dry cider
3–4 tablespoons plain flour	240 ml (8 fl oz) chicken
30–45 g (1–1½ oz) butter	stock, or more
240 g (8 oz) small button	Bouquet garni
mushrooms, stems trimmed	4–5 tablespoons
2 leeks, finely sliced	crème fraîche

1 Cut the rabbit into eight serving pieces. Season with salt and pepper and coat lightly with flour

2 Melt half the butter over medium-high heat in a large casserole. Add the rabbit pieces and brown them, cooking in batches and adding more butter, if necessary. Remove the meat when browned.

3 Melt the remaining butter in the same pan, add the mushrooms and sauté until well coloured. Add the leeks and carrot and cook for 1–2 minutes. Return the rabbit pieces to the casserole. Stir in the cider and bring to the boil. Pour on the stock, adding more if needed, so it just covers the meat. Add the bouquet garni and simmer very gently over low heat, covered, for an hour, or until the rabbit is very tender and the juices run clear when the thickest part of the meat is pierced with a knife. (Wild rabbit may take longer.) Remove to a warm serving platter and keep warm.

4 Skim off any fat from the cooking liquid, stir in the cream and simmer for 4–5 minutes. Taste and adjust the seasoning and strain the sauce. Coat the rabbit pieces with some of the sauce and serve the rest separately.

Pintade au Chou à la Normande

GUINEA FOWL WITH CABBAGE AND APPLES

Apples and cabbage have a wonderful affinity. They are perfect partnered with the plump, juicy guinea fowl and local cider you find in the farmers' markets in rural Normandy.

SERVES 4

1.5 kg (3 lb) guinea fowl
15 g (½ oz) butter
1 large onion, halved and sliced
1 large leek, sliced
500 g (1 lb) green cabbage, sliced
2 cooking apples, cored and sliced
Salt and pepper
120 ml (4 fl oz) dry cider
120 ml (4 fl oz) chicken stock
1–2 garlic cloves, finely chopped

1 Preheat the oven to 180°C/350°F/Gas Mark 4. Truss the guinea fowl.

2 Heat half the butter in a heavy casserole over medium-high heat. Sauté the guinea fowl until golden brown, turning to colour it evenly. Remove when browned.

3 Pour out the fat and add the remaining butter to the casserole. Reduce the heat to low and stir in the onion and leek. Cook for 5 minutes, stirring occasionally, add the cabbage and cook for a few minutes, until slightly wilted. Stir in the apple slices and season to taste with salt and pepper. Place the guinea fowl, breast-side down, on the vegetable mixture.

4 Pour over the cider and bring to the boil, then add the stock and garlic. Cover the casserole and transfer to the oven. Cook for 50 minutes, or until the vegetables and guinea fowl are tender, turning the bird over halfway through the cooking time.

5 To serve, cut the guinea fowl into 4 or 8 pieces. Transfer the cabbage and apples to a serving platter, using a slotted spoon, and arrange the guinea fowl joints on top. Serve the cooking juices separately.

Faisan à la Normande

PHEASANT WITH APPLES, CALVADOS AND CREAM

This is a perfect way to serve pheasant. The lean meat is kept moist during cooking and the rich Normandy cream and tangy cider produce a wonderfully balanced sauce, redolent of apples.

SERVES 4–5

45 g (1½ oz) butter
4 tart apples, about 500 g
(1 lb), peeled, cored and
cut in eighths
2 oven-ready pheasants,
about 875 g (1¾ lb) each
Salt and pepper

2 shallots, finely chopped
3 tablespoons Calvados
360 ml (12 fl oz) dry cider
Bouquet garni
2 teaspoons cornflour
180 ml (6 fl oz) crème fraîche
or double cream

1 Melt two-thirds of the butter in a heavy frying pan over medium heat and sauté the apple pieces until lightly browned, turning them frequently to colour evenly.

2 Season the pheasants inside and out with salt and pepper. Put the apples into the cavities of the birds, dividing them evenly, and tie the legs with string. Preheat the oven to 200°C/400°F/Gas Mark 6.

3 Over medium-high heat, melt the remaining butter in a heavy flameproof casserole large enough to hold both birds. Brown the pheasants, turning them 3 or 4 times to colour evenly and ending breast-side up. Add the shallots and cook for 1–2 minutes more, pushing them under the birds. Pour over the Calvados, and then the cider. Bring to the boil, add the bouquet garni and place a piece of greaseproof paper or foil over the breasts. Cover tightly and transfer to the oven.

4 Cook the pheasants for 25–30 minutes, basting twice, or until the juices that run out are faintly pink when the thickest part of the thigh is pierced with a skewer. Remove the birds to a serving platter or carving board and cover them loosely with foil to keep them warm.

5 Strain the cooking juices and remove the fat. Pour back into the casserole and boil to reduce the liquid by about one-third. Stir the cornflour into the cream and add to the cooking liquid. Boil, stirring frequently, for 2–3 minutes, until slightly thickened. Carve the pheasants and serve with the sauce.

Cailles au Cidre et au Vinaigre

QUAILS WITH ONIONS, CIDER AND CIDER VINEGAR

Cider vinegar is often available flavoured with herbs or even honey.
Adjust the amount used in the recipe according to the strength of the vinegar
– it should balance the sweetness of the onion.

SERVES 4

8 ready-to-cook quails, about
150 g (5 oz) each
Salt and pepper
30 g (1 oz) butter
2 large, sweet onions,
halved and sliced
2 garlic cloves,
finely chopped

3–4 tablespoons cider vinegar
150 ml (¼ pint) dry cider
150 ml (¼ pint) chicken stock
Bouquet garni
1½ teaspoons cornflour,
dissolved in
1 tablespoon water

1 Season the quails inside and out with salt and pepper and tie the legs with string.

2 Melt half the butter in a large, heavy casserole over medium-high heat and brown the birds, turning them from one side of the breast to the other, to the back; cook them in batches if necessary. Remove when browned.

3 Melt the remaining butter and add the onions. Cover and cook over medium-low heat for about 5 minutes until soft, stirring occasionally. Uncover and continue cooking, stirring frequently, until deep golden brown, about 15 more minutes. Add the garlic and cook for 2 minutes, stirring. Add the cider vinegar and boil for a minute.

4 Return the quails to the casserole and add the cider and stock. Bring to the boil, add the bouquet garni and cover tightly. Reduce the heat and simmer gently for 20 minutes, or until the quails are cooked through. Remove them, cut off the trussing string and keep them warm, loosely covered.

5 Bring the sauce to the boil, add the dissolved cornflour and boil for 3 minutes, stirring frequently, until the sauce is slightly syrupy. Strain it into a sauceboat. Make a bed of the onions on a warm platter. Arrange the quails on top, pour over a little sauce and serve the remainder separately.

Beautiful scenery, like this peaceful view of Château Lassay, draws visitors to Normandy as much as the superb local cuisine.

45

Pavé de Chevreuil au Camembert

VENISON STEAK WITH CAMEMBERT CHEESE

*This recipe pairs the product for which the Orne is best known – Camembert cheese –
with rich, flavourful venison. Wild deer roam the forests here, but they are also
farmed near Argentan, not far from the village of Camembert.*

SERVES 4

4 venison sirloin
steaks, about 150–180 g
(5–6 oz) each
Salt and pepper
1 garlic clove, peeled and
finely chopped
4 tablespoons Calvados
15 g (½ oz) butter

3 tablespoons dry cider
120–150 ml (4–5 fl oz) crème
fraîche or whipping cream
1½ teaspoons Dijon mustard
½ Camembert cheese, about
120 g (4 oz), rind removed
(75 g (2½ oz) without rind)

1 If you wish, place the steaks between sheets of greaseproof paper and beat them with a rolling pin to tenderize them. Put the steaks in a shallow ceramic or glass dish just large enough to hold them, sprinkle them generously with pepper, spread the garlic on them and pour over the Calvados. Leave to stand for 20–30 minutes, turning once.

2 Melt the butter in a heavy frying pan over medium-high heat. When it is foamy, add the venison, reserving the marinade. Cook for about 2–3 minutes per side, or until done as preferred. Remove the meat and keep warm.

3 Pour the reserved Calvados marinade into the pan, add the cider and bring to the boil, stirring and scraping the bottom of the pan. Stir in the cream and bring back to the boil. Add the mustard and cheese and stir until smooth.

4 Pour any accumulated juices from the meat into the sauce and add more cream if it seems thick. Adjust the seasoning and serve the sauce over the meat.

Camembert, a tiny village, is the birthplace of the famous cheese.

Magret de Canard aux Pommes et à la Crème

DUCK BREAST WITH APPLES AND CREAM SAUCE

This dish incorporates quintessential Normandy produce -- apples, cream and Calvados. Use large, meaty Duclair duck breasts if you can find them. If the duck breasts are small, you will need one per person.

SERVES 4

2 eating apples, quartered, cored and peeled
30 g (1 oz) butter
Salt and pepper
2 large duck breasts, about 360 g (12 oz) each, skin removed

4 tablespoons Calvados
180 ml (6 fl oz) double or whipping cream
1 teaspoon Dijon mustard

1 Cut each apple quarter into three slices (or two slices if the apples are small). Heat half the butter in a large non-stick frying pan and add the apples. Cook over moderate heat, stirring frequently, until the apples are light golden brown, about 12 minutes. Set aside.

2 Heat the remaining butter in a heavy frying pan. Season the duck breasts on both sides and cook over medium-high heat for 2 minutes per side. Remove and keep warm, loosely covered with foil.

3 Add the Calvados to the frying pan, boil briefly and add the cream. Boil for 2–3 minutes, until the sauce thickens slightly, stirring and scraping up the browned bits from the bottom of the pan. Stir in the mustard. Taste and add salt and pepper as needed.

4 Pour any accumulated juices from the breasts into the pan. To serve, slice the meat crosswise on the diagonal, arrange it on a serving platter, garnish with the sautéd apple slices and pour the sauce over.

Cook's Notes

Duck breasts often come with a thick, fatty skin, which is removed for this recipe. If you wish, cut the skin into thin strips and fry over moderate heat until brown and crisp to make "cracklings". Drain and use like bacon, for garnishing or in salads.

Normandy's climate makes it particularly suited to the cultivation of vegetables. Mild winters, warm summers and adequate to abundant rain favour many vegetables; carrots, leeks, cauliflower and potatoes are among the most important crops. One large co-op, *Jardins de Normandie*, proclaims its harvests to be the "cream of fresh vegetables", a subtle reference to Normandy's most renowned product, and emphasizes the availability of its vegetables throughout the year.

New season's garlic is wonderfully mild and can be used like spring onions.

Early vegetables profit from the moderating influence of the Gulf stream and the moisture in the sea air. In the Manche, fields stretch nearly to the edge of the sea and at harvest time the coastal roads are clogged with lorries full of cauliflowers or cabbages. Farming here is a profitable enterprise and the younger generation often elects to stay on the land rather than join the exodus to the cities.

Créances, in the centre of the western coast of the Manche, can boast of the only carrots to be granted AOC recognition – the same system by which wines and cheeses are authenticated. These carrots are grown in salty, sandy soil and nourished with seaweed instead of chemicals. They are bright orange and perfectly shaped, with no core, so there is no waste. With sequential planting, they are harvested most of the year, except in midsummer. The co-operative handles grading

Vegetables and salads

and distribution for the numerous small and larger producers. This kind of collective effort is one of the reasons that makes farming smallholdings worthwhile. Leek fields adjoin carrot fields around Créances. Leeks flourish in many parts of Normandy and play an important role in agricultural commerce. Root vegetables, such as celeriac, turnips and premium early potatoes, are also major components of Normandy's great vegetable basket, along with onions, garlic and shallots. Pale, plump heads of chicory and various kinds of salad leaves and herbs luxuriate in the mild temperatures.

Smaller farmers often sell their vegetables locally at the colourful weekly markets held all over Normandy. Many of the stall holders move around a circuit of markets, offering their produce in different places each day of the week, but you will also find local farmers bringing in the overflow from their own kitchen gardens. An overturned crate becomes an impromptu market stall, with a few heads of glistening lettuce, bunches of young chard, perhaps a few flowers and a basket of eggs on display.

Beetroot and sugar beet thrive in the chalky soil of the *Pays de Caux*, where rows of trees planted along country roads filter the winds that sweep across this wide plateau. In France, beetroot usually comes to market already cooked, so it is easy to use in salads and only needs reheating when served as a hot vegetable.

In Normandy, cooked vegetables are often laced with a little cream or coated with a typical sauce made of cider and cream, *sauce Normande*. This versatile sauce is especially good with cauliflower or leeks. It is also traditionally served with fish and sometimes poultry; when served with a main course, it often contains sliced mushrooms.

Farmers of small holdings often bring surplus produce to sell at the market.

Wild mushrooms are found in many parts of Normandy. In fact, *cèpes* are more prolific in the Orne than in Périgord, which is better known for them, but the Orne's residents prefer to keep quiet about that. For some people, mushroom-hunting is not just a pleasant way to spend time in the woods. With an ever-growing demand for wild mushrooms from restaurateurs and markets, it can be lucrative.

The French custom of daily shopping and using produce in season has created a continual demand for fresh vegetables, salad leaves and herbs. In Normandy, agricultural traditions have been successfully combined with modern commercial considerations and regional recipes still celebrate local products.

Fresh herbs are widely available in French markets and greengrocers' shops.

Brioches aux Champignons Sauvages

WILD MUSHROOMS IN BRIOCHES

The Orne is great mushroom-hunting territory – in the forests near Longny-au-Perche and in the Andaines forest, where one of the local hostelries sometimes offers tutored excursions in search of wild fungi.

The selection of wild mushrooms on this market stall is superb.

Cook's Notes

If preferred, serve the mushrooms on four slices of lightly toasted brioche instead of in individual brioches.

SERVES 4

600 g (1¼ lb) fresh wild mushrooms, or mixed wild and cultivated mushrooms
30 g (1 oz) butter, melted
2 shallots, finely chopped
150 ml (¼ pint) crème fraîche or double cream

Salt and pepper
2 tablespoons chopped fresh parsley
4 individual brioches, warmed in a low oven

1 Trim the mushroom stems and wipe the mushrooms with a damp cloth or, if necessary, rinse under cool running water and carefully pat dry. Cut the mushrooms into quarters or slices.

2 Heat the butter in a large, heavy frying pan over medium-high heat, until foamy. Add the mushrooms and cook for 4–5 minutes, until they have given off some liquid. Add the shallots and cook for 4–5 minutes more, until the mushrooms are tender and lightly browned and the liquid has evaporated. Add the cream and season to taste with salt and pepper. Stir in the parsley.

3 Slice the tops from the brioches, cutting down toward the centre so there will be an indentation when the tops are removed. Remove the tops and trim off the part that came from the interior. Place the brioche bottoms on four warm plates, spoon the mushrooms and sauce over them, dividing it evenly, and set the tops on at an angle.

Pommes de Terre Nouvelles à la Crème d'Oseille

NEW POTATOES WITH SORREL CREAM SAUCE

Fresh sorrel lends a wonderful tanginess to these creamy potatoes.

SERVES 4

500 g (1 lb) small new potatoes, scrubbed or peeled
180 ml (6 fl oz) crème fraîche or double cream
1–2 garlic cloves, finely chopped

150 g (5 oz) small fresh sorrel leaves, stems removed, washed and blotted dry

1 Put the potatoes into salted water, bring to the boil over medium-high heat, reduce the heat to medium and boil gently until just tender, 12–15 minutes. Drain.

2 In a saucepan, combine the cream and garlic and set over medium heat, until bubbles appear around the edge. Reduce the heat to low and leave to simmer for about 15 minutes, or until slightly thickened.

3 Add the sorrel to the cream mixture. Cook, stirring constantly, until the sorrel is completely melted. Add the potatoes, stir to coat and simmer until heated through.

Choufleur Sauce Normande

CAULIFLOWER WITH CIDER CREAM SAUCE

This classic Norman cider sauce is often used on vegetables, but also on fish,
shellfish and poultry – in fact, just about anything. When the sauce is served with
fish or shellfish, it usually includes their cooking liquid.

SERVES 4

30 g (1 oz) butter
20 g (¾ oz) plain flour
120 ml (4 fl oz) dry cider
180 ml (6 fl oz) crème fraîche
Salt and pepper
Freshly grated nutmeg

Bay leaf
1 cauliflower,
about 420 g
(14 oz)
Chopped fresh parsley,
to garnish

1 Melt the butter in a saucepan over medium heat. Stir in the flour and cook for 2 minutes. Add the cider and whisk vigorously until smooth. Reduce the heat to low, stir in the cream and add salt, pepper and nutmeg to taste, with the bay leaf. Simmer, stirring occasionally, for 12–15 minutes. Adjust the seasoning, if needed, and remove the bay leaf.

2 If you wish, break the cauliflower into florets. Steam, tightly covered, until tender. Serve with the cider sauce and garnish with a little parsley.

Carottes et Echalotes Etuvées au Beurre

GLAZED CARROTS AND SHALLOTS

The carrots that grow in the sandy soil of the Cotentin peninsula have a special salty flavour that comes from the seaweed used to enrich the soil and the proximity of the fields to the sea. They are perfect paired with sweet local shallots.

SERVES 4

500 g (1 lb) medium
carrots, peeled
30 g (1 oz) butter
240 g (8 oz) small
shallots, peeled

120 ml (4 fl oz) chicken or
vegetable stock or water
1–2 teaspoons caster sugar

1 Cut the carrots into pieces about 2 cm (¾ inch) long.

2 Melt the butter in a heavy saucepan over medium heat. Add the carrots and shallots and stir to combine.

3 Add the chicken or vegetable stock or water and bring to the boil over medium-high heat. Cover the pan and cook over medium heat for about 10 minutes, stirring occasionally, until the vegetables begin to soften.

4 Uncover the pan and sprinkle with sugar. Increase the heat to medium-high and cook uncovered, stirring frequently, until the remaining liquid has evaporated and the vegetables are glazed.

Market stalls have beautiful displays of produce, such as these vegetables.

Blettes à la Crème

SWISS CHARD WITH CREAM

I first made this recipe one blustery day after a visit to the local market, where I found tender new chard leaves and wonderful raw cream, so thick it would hardly fall from the ladle.

SERVES 4

A bunch of young Swiss chard, about 500 g (1 lb), well rinsed and blotted dry
240 ml (8 fl oz) double cream

Salt and pepper
Freshly grated nutmeg
2–3 tablespoons grated Gruyère cheese

1 Cut off the chard stems at the bottom of the leaves and slice the stems into 1 cm (½-inch) pieces. Slice the leaves across into thin ribbons.

2 Bring a pan of salted water to the boil over high heat and drop in the chard stems. When the water comes back to the boil, drain the stems and gently blot them dry on paper towels.

3 Preheat the oven to 180°C/350°F/Gas Mark 4. In a heavy saucepan, bring the cream to a boil over medium-high heat and season with salt, pepper and nutmeg. Add the chard leaves and stir until wilted, about 4 minutes. Stir in the chard stems. Transfer to a gratin dish and sprinkle with the grated cheese. Bake for about 20 minutes, or until bubbly and browned on top.

Cook's Notes

If using very large chard leaves, with ribs more than 2.5 cm (1 inch) wide, you may prefer to peel the ribs with a vegetable peeler and to cut the rib extensions out of the leaves.

Market day is the high point of the week in many villages.

Gratin de Poireaux et de Pommes de Terre

LEEK AND POTATO GRATIN

This satisfying dish – which highlights some of Normandy's most prolifically cultivated vegetables and the dairy produce for which it is even better known – is perfect for winter suppers or as an accompaniment to roast poultry or meat.

SERVES 4–8

750 g (1½ lb) potatoes, peeled and thinly sliced
600 ml (1 pint) milk
Salt and pepper
Freshly grated nutmeg
1 bay leaf

15 g (½ oz) butter
500 g (1 lb) leeks, thinly sliced
300 ml (½ pint) whipping cream

1 Preheat the oven to 180°C/350°F/Gas Mark 4. Generously butter a 36 cm (14-inch) oval gratin dish or a 2-litre (3¼ pint) shallow baking dish.

2 Put the potatoes in a large saucepan and pour over the milk. Add salt and pepper, nutmeg and bay leaf. Simmer over medium heat, stirring occasionally, until the potatoes are nearly tender but not completely cooked.

3 Meanwhile, melt the butter in a saucepan over medium heat. Add the leeks, cover and cook, stirring frequently, until they are wilted but not browned. Add 240 ml (8 fl oz) of the cream and cook gently until the leeks are completely wilted, about 15 minutes. Season with more salt and pepper.

4 Using a slotted spoon, transfer half of the potatoes to the prepared dish. Top with the leek and cream mixture and cover with the remaining potatoes. Pour over enough of the milk from the potatoes to come just below the surface of the potatoes. Film the top with the remaining cream and bake until golden, about an hour.

Salade Cauchoise

NORMANDY POTATO SALAD

The chalky soil that characterizes the Pays de Caux *makes it ideal for the cultivation of potatoes. This regional potato salad seems to have many versions – try adding apple, or using small peeled, cooked prawns instead of ham.*

SERVES 4

120 g (4 oz) small button mushrooms, stems removed
3 tablespoons dry cider or lemon juice
6 tablespoons crème fraîche
Salt and white pepper
360 g (12 oz) medium waxy potatoes

3 tablespoons cider vinegar
2 celery sticks, thinly sliced or diced
120 g (4 oz) cooked ham, cut in strips
2 tablespoons snipped fresh chives, plus more to garnish

1 Slice the mushrooms thinly and put them in a bowl. Add the cider or lemon juice and half the cream. Stir gently to mix. Season to taste and let stand for an hour or more, stirring once or twice.

2 Meanwhile, put the potatoes, unpeeled, into salted water and bring to the boil over medium-high heat. Reduce the heat to medium and boil the potatoes gently until tender, about 15–20 minutes. Drain.

3 When cool enough to handle, peel the potatoes and cut them in 1.5 cm (⅝-inch) cubes. Sprinkle with cider vinegar and toss.

4 Combine the mushrooms and their dressing, the potatoes, celery and ham. Add the remaining cream and the chives and toss to combine well. Adjust the seasoning, if needed, and serve at room temperature or chill until serving. Garnish with more chives.

Salade de Betteraves au Vinaigrette de Noisette

BEETROOT SALAD WITH HAZELNUT VINAIGRETTE

Products from the same region are often good in combination – as in this tasty salad.

SERVES 4

2 teaspoons cider vinegar
3 tablespoons hazelnut oil
Salt and pepper
2 tablespoons chopped
fresh chives
180 g (6 oz) cooked
beetroot, peeled

360 g (12 oz) chicory
Small bunch of watercress,
stems removed
Duck cracklings, to garnish
(see Cook's Notes, page 47),
optional

1 In a medium bowl, whisk together the vinegar, oil, salt and pepper to taste and half the chives.

2 Dice the beetroot, put it in a small bowl and toss with one-third of the dressing.

3 Cut the chicory into thin slices and add to the remaining dressing, with the watercress leaves. Toss to coat thoroughly.

4 Arrange the chicory and watercress on a serving plate and mound the beetroot in the centre, or divide the components among four individual salad plates, and sprinkle over the remaining chives. Garnish with duck cracklings, if you wish.

Hazelnuts are pressed to make an aromatic oil, delicious in salads.

While they are often enjoyed as separate courses, free-range eggs and well matured cheese have an elegance and versatility when combined, as in a soufflé or quiche.

Cheese has been made in Normandy since the eleventh century. The dark brown-and-white dappled Normandy cattle, with their distinctive eye patches, have now been joined by Friesians and the milkmaid has in most cases been replaced by a machine, but dairy-farming is still one of Normandy's main industries. More than any other region of France, Normandy is associated with dairy produce: milk, cream,

Eggs and Cheese

butter and, especially, cheese. France produces more kinds of cheese than any other country and General de Gaulle was once heard to complain about the impossibility of governing a country which produced 324 different kinds of cheese. Of the 32 cheeses now entitled to AOC status (*Appellation d'Origine Contrôlée*), Normandy can claim four of these, *Camembert, Pont-l'Evêque, Livarot* and *Neufchâtel*, as well as many others including *Pavé d'Auge, Lisieux, Trouville* and among the newer cheeses, triple-cream *Brillat-Savarin* and *Coutances*.

Pont-l'Evêque cheese has been in existence since the early twelfth century, when it was made by monks. This highly aromatic, washed-rind cheese is moulded in a square shape. The golden rind encloses a rich, slightly runny interior and, although the aroma is potent, the flavour of this cheese is not as strong as you might expect. An annual contest

Rich milk and cream from Normandy's dairy herds makes superb cheeses.

for the best *Pont-l'Evêque* takes place in May, in the town of the same name.

Livarot, equally, is one of Normandy's oldest cheeses. Another washed-rind cheese, the fairly dark rind tinged with rust colour is encircled with reeds (or paper) to keep its round shape. It has a distinctive, strong aroma and a creamy interior which, while stronger than *Pont-l'Evêque*, is relatively mild; most of the pungency comes from the rind. Today this cheese is rarely, if ever, made on farms: most comes from commercial dairies, but the traditional standards have been maintained and *Livarot* was the first Normandy cheese to be awarded AOC status. The cheese museum in Livarot is a must for gastronomic travellers.

Neufchâtel, which dates back to 1035, might today look like a commercial cheese, but much of it is made by farmers' wives. Over 40 farms around Neufchâtel-en-Bray produce this tangy cheese in various formats, the most memorable being heart-shaped, either large or small, but large and small rectangular and cylindrical shapes are also to be found. The Saturday market in the town offers a wide choice of farmhouse cheeses.

Camembert-style cheeses are made all over the world, but the real thing is only made in Normandy and must be ladled into the mould. It is not improved by pasteurization, so the best examples are those made from raw milk – look for "*au lait cru*" on the label – within the area specified in its AOC, which was only granted in 1983. The *fête du Camembert*, held at the end of July, celebrates one of France's best loved cheeses.

THE STORY OF CAMEMBERT

Records indicate that Vimoutiers was a source for a cheese similar to *Camembert* in the late 1600s, a century before the French Revolution. Regarding the origin of *Camembert*, the story goes that in 1790, Marie Herel, an inhabitant of the small village of Camembert near Vimoutiers, sheltered a priest fleeing from the revolution. He had learned how to produce soft-ripened cheese in the area around Brie and divulged the secret of the maturation to his benefactress. She capitalized on his advice, using the abundant, rich Normandy milk, and began to sell *Camembert* commercially in local markets by the following year. Napoleon III took a fancy to the cheese and its popularity soared. A century after its launch came a development crucial to the shipment of this cheese: the wooden boxes, which were invented by Ridel in 1890 and which are still in use, made

widespread distribution a viable option. This increased the popularity of *Camembert* even further, aided by the improvement in rail transport. Today, only two farms are actually making cheese in the village, the bulk of the production having been shifted to other locations.

Soufflé au Livarot

LIVAROT CHEESE SOUFFLÉ

Livarot is one of four Normandy cheeses given a special Appellation
Contrôlée *classification, which it received in 1975. The washed rind of
this cheese gives it a pungent aroma, but the interior is surprisingly mild.*

SERVES 4 (OR 6 AS A STARTER)

Grated Parmesan cheese,
for sprinkling
30 g (1 oz) butter
30 g (1 oz) plain flour
210 ml (7 fl oz) milk
Bay leaf
Salt and pepper
Freshly grated nutmeg

3 eggs, at room
temperature, separated
1 small Livarot cheese, about
240 g (8 oz), rind removed,
cut in small pieces
2 egg whites, at
room temperature
¼ teaspoon cream of tartar

1 Preheat the oven to 190°C/375°F/Gas Mark 5. Lightly grease a 1.5-litre (2½-pint) soufflé dish and sprinkle with Parmesan cheese.

2 Melt the butter in a heavy saucepan over medium heat. Add the flour, stir to blend and cook for 3 minutes, stirring occasionally. Pour in half the milk, stirring vigorously until smooth, then stir in the remaining milk and add the bay leaf. Season with a pinch of salt and plenty of pepper and nutmeg. Reduce the heat to low, cover and simmer gently for about 5 minutes, stirring occasionally. Remove the sauce from the heat and discard the bay leaf. Stir in the egg yolks, one at a time, and the Livarot cheese.

3 Put the egg whites and cream of tartar in a large bowl. Using an electric mixer, beat slowly until the mixture becomes frothy. Increase the speed gradually to moderately high and continue beating until firm peaks form.

4 Stir a spoonful of beaten egg whites into the cheese sauce to lighten it. Pour the sauce over the whites and, using a large rubber spatula or metal spoon, quickly and lightly fold until they are just combined.

5 Turn the soufflé mixture into the prepared dish and run your finger around the edge of the mixture. Bake for about 25 minutes until puffed and golden brown on top. Serve immediately.

Fresh eggs and local cheese make a memorable combination.

Tartlettes au Neufchâtel

NEUFCHÂTEL CHEESE AND SPINACH TARTLETS

Neufchâtel cheese is often made by small artisanal producers, as well as by larger industrial concerns. If you are travelling in the Seine-Maritime, follow the signs for the route du fromage de Neufchâtel *and call in to see the cheese being made.*

SERVES 4

210 g (7 oz) leaf spinach, stems removed, rinsed	2 Neufchâtel cheeses, 210 g (7 oz) each heart-shaped if possible
2 eggs	
150 ml (¼ pint) single cream	240 g (8 oz) filo pastry, about 6 sheets
Salt and pepper	
Freshly grated nutmeg	60 g (2 oz) melted butter

Cook's Notes

If you prefer, substitute a fairly firm goat's cheese, such as those now made in Normandy, for the Neufchâtel cheeses.

1 Preheat the oven to 190°C/375°F/Gas Mark 5. Lightly butter four 13 cm (5-inch) tartlet tins. Put a baking sheet large enough to hold the tartlet tins into the oven.

2 Steam the spinach until wilted (or microwave it according to manufacturer's guidelines). Drain it and squeeze it dry by small handfuls. Put the spinach in a food processor or blender and purée it. Add the eggs and cream and mix until combined. Season to taste with salt, pepper and nutmeg.

3 Using a plate as a guide, cut 16 rounds 18 cm (7 inches) in diameter from the filo pastry. (Do this while the sheets of pastry are stacked. Cover the cut rounds to prevent the pastry from drying out.) Working with four rounds at a time, brush with butter and layer four rounds in each of the tins.

4 Cut the cheeses in half crossways. Put a piece of cheese, cut-side up, in the bottom of each mould. Place the moulds on the preheated baking sheet and carefully pour or spoon the spinach cream around the cheeses. Bake until puffed and golden, about 30 minutes. Serve the tartlets hot or warm.

Tourte Augeronne au Livarot et au Pont l'Eveque

CHEESE TART WITH LIVAROT AND PONT L'EVÊQUE

This regional tart is like a rich, firm quiche. Serve it with green salad.

SERVES 4 (OR 6 AS A STARTER)

240 g (8 oz) butter shortcrust pastry (see page 78)
1 small Livarot cheese, about 240 g (8 oz), rind removed
½ Pont l'Evêque, about 210 g (7 oz), rind removed

1 egg
3 tablespoons crème fraîche
100 ml (3½ fl oz) milk
Freshly ground pepper
Freshly grated nutmeg

1 Roll out the pastry dough to a thickness of about 6 mm (¼ inch) and line a 23 cm (9-inch) tart tin. Chill for 15–30 minutes. Preheat the oven to 200°C/400°F/Gas Mark 6.

2 Lightly prick the bottom of the pastry case and line it with foil. Fill the foil with dried beans or baking weights to make a thick layer and bake for 15 minutes, until the edge is slightly dry and set. Remove the foil and beans and continue baking for 5 minutes.

3 Using a food processor or sturdy fork, mash together the cheeses, egg and cream until homogenous. Gradually add the milk and mix until smooth. Season with pepper and nutmeg.

4 Pour the cheese mixture into the pastry case, level it and bake for about 25 minutes, until it is puffed and well browned. Remove to a wire rack and leave to cool for 10–12 minutes before serving.

Croque Normande

TOASTED SANDWICHES WITH HAM AND NORMANDY CHEESE

Toasted sandwiches are typical fare in French cafés and bars. This combination features some of Normandy's finest products and it's certainly a cut above the standard croque monsieur.

SERVES 4

Butter, for spreading
8 rectangular slices of brioche
120 g (4 oz) thinly sliced
country ham

240 g (8 oz) Pont l'Evêque,
Camembert or Livarot
cheese, crust removed if
wished, sliced

1 Preheat the grill to hot. Set a large frying pan over medium-low heat. Lightly butter the brioche slices.

2 Arrange the ham on the unbuttered sides of four brioche slices, dividing it evenly. Top with the remaining brioche slices, buttered-side up. Cook the sandwiches in the frying pan until lightly browned on both sides, turning once.

3 Transfer the sandwiches to a baking tray or grill pan, arrange the cheese slices over the tops and grill until the cheese melts.

Informal cafés like this can provide a pleasant pause in the day.

Crêpes au Petit Suisse et aux Poireaux

CRÊPES WITH SOFT CHEESE AND LEEKS

The delicate filling in these crêpes features Petit-Suisse, an unsalted, soft, fresh cheese produced on a large scale in the Pays de Bray. If necessary, substitute salted soft cheese and reduce or omit the salt from the seasoning.

SERVES 4

15 g (½ oz) butter
360 g (12 oz) small leeks, thinly sliced
100 ml (3½ fl oz) whipping cream
210 g (7 oz) soft cheese, unsalted if possible
180 g (6 oz) lean cooked ham, diced
1 tablespoon chopped fresh tarragon
Salt and pepper

Freshly grated nutmeg
3–4 tablespoons grated Gruyère or Parmesan cheese

FOR THE CRÊPES
120 g (4 oz) plain flour
Pinch of salt
2 eggs
180 ml (6 fl oz) milk
5 tablespoons water
30 g (1 oz) melted butter, plus more for frying

1 For the crêpes, sift the flour and salt into a bowl and make a well in the centre. Whisk together the eggs, milk and water and slowly pour them into the well, whisking constantly and gradually bringing in the flour until a smooth batter forms. Whisk in 2 tablespoons of melted butter and let the batter stand for about 20 minutes. If the batter thickens, add a little water to thin it. (The batter should have the consistency of cream.)

Cook's Notes

For a seafood variation, substitute cooked, peeled small prawns or mussels for the ham.

2 To cook the crêpes, set a 20 cm (8-inch) crêpe pan over medium-high heat. Brush the pan with a little melted butter. Stir the batter, ladle about 2 tablespoons of it into the pan and quickly tilt the pan to cover the bottom with a thin layer of batter. Cook until bubbles appear on the top, about a minute; then turn over and cook for 20–30 seconds more, until golden. Turn on to a plate and continue cooking the crêpes, brushing the pan with melted butter as necessary. Stack the crêpes between sheets of greaseproof paper.

3 Preheat the oven to 190°C/375°F/Gas Mark 5.

4 For the filling, melt the butter in a saucepan and cook the leeks, partially covered, over medium heat, until softened but not browned, about 10 minutes, stirring frequently. Add the cream and cook gently until the leeks are completely soft and the cream has thickened a little, about 5 minutes. Stir in the soft cheese, ham and tarragon and cook gently until the cheese melts. Season with salt, pepper and nutmeg.

5 Put 2–3 tablespoons of filling on one side of each crêpe and roll up. Arrange the crêpes in a lightly buttered baking dish, sprinkle with grated cheese and bake until heated through, about 10 minutes.

Pain au Camembert

CAMEMBERT BREAD

This aromatic bread is a bit like cheesy brioche, although it is firmer and more crusty than brioche. A food processor makes it easy to work in the cheese. If you wish, you can bake the bread in small brioche moulds or even in a large one.

MAKES 1 LOAF OR 8 ROLLS

2 tablespoons warm milk
½ teaspoon caster sugar
2 teaspoons instant dry yeast
240 g (8 oz) plain flour
¼ teaspoon salt
2 eggs

30 g (1 oz) butter, melted
120 g (4 oz) Camembert cheese, crust removed, cut in about 10 pieces
beaten egg, for glazing

Neighbourhood bakeries ensure a ready source of fresh bread.

1 Combine the warm milk, sugar and yeast in a small bowl. Stir until dissolved and leave to stand for 2–3 minutes, or until the yeast starts to bubble.

2 Put the flour and salt into a food processor fitted with a plastic blade, or a metal one, and pulse to combine.

3 Beat the egg and melted butter into the yeast mixture. With the machine running, slowly pour it through the feed tube and process until well combined and the dough looks curdy. Scrape down the sides and add the cheese. Continue processing until the dough comes together into a ball.

4 Transfer the dough to a lightly floured surface and knead it 10–20 times.

5 Generously butter a loaf tin or eight individual brioche moulds. Shape the dough into a cylinder or into eight balls and put into the tin or moulds. Leave to prove in a warm place until doubled in bulk. (To determine if the dough has risen enough, press lightly with your finger; when the indentation stays, the dough is ready to bake.)

6 Meanwhile, preheat the oven to 190°C/375°F/Gas Mark 5. Glaze the bread with the beaten egg and bake until deep golden brown, about 30 minutes for a loaf or 15 minutes for individual moulds. Cool on a rack.

Oeufs en Cocotte Marie Herel

BAKED EGGS WITH CAMEMBERT CHEESE

*This dish is named for the "inventor" of Camembert cheese. When the cheese melts,
it makes a creamy sauce for the eggs. Serve with toast soldiers or slim pieces of
toasted brioche for dipping.*

SERVES 4

100 g (3½ oz) Camembert
cheese without rind, sliced
4 eggs
4 tablespoons double or
whipping cream

Salt and freshly
ground pepper
Freshly grated nutmeg

1 Preheat the oven to 190°C/375°F/Gas Mark 5. Lightly butter four ramekins or individual soufflé dishes.

2 Arrange the slices of Camembert in the bottom of the dishes, dividing them evenly. Press them down to cover the bottom evenly. Break an egg into each dish and pour a tablespoon of cream over each egg. Season lightly with salt, pepper and nutmeg.

3 Put the ramekins into a shallow baking dish and pour in boiling water to come halfway up the sides. Bake for about 10 minutes, until the white is set and the yolk still soft, or longer if you prefer them more set.

Oeufs Brouíllés aux Crevettes

SCRAMBLED EGGS WITH PRAWNS

*Only small prawns will be warmed through by the heat of the eggs,
so the tiny prawns from Honfleur are best for this. Peeling them is a bit
tedious, but the flavour makes it a worthwhile task.*

SERVES 4

40 g (1½ oz) butter, cut
in small pieces
8 eggs
Salt and pepper
150 g (5 oz) small cooked,
peeled prawns

1 tablespoon crème fraîche
1–2 tablespoons chopped
fresh chives

1 In a large, heavy saucepan, melt half the butter over medium-low heat.

2 Beat the eggs with salt and pepper to taste. Pour into the saucepan and cook very gently for about 10 minutes, stirring constantly with a whisk or wooden spoon, until the egg mixture begins to thicken and set. Gradually stir in the remaining pieces of butter, lifting the pan from the heat occasionally to slow the cooking.

3 When the eggs are nearly set, stir in the prawns and cook only long enough to heat through, about a minute. Take the pan from the heat and stir in the cream, to stop the cooking. Divide the scrambled egg mixture evenly among four warm ramekins or scallop shells and sprinkle with chives.

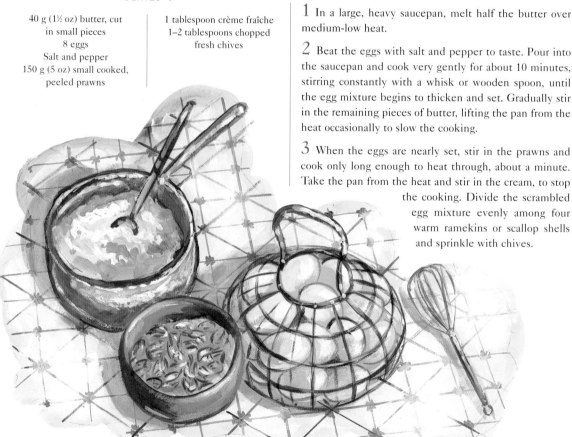

Omelette Mère Poulard

SOUFFLÉ-OMELETTE MÈRE POULARDE

This signature dish of the renowned restaurant at the foot of Mont-Saint-Michel abbey is cooked over an open fire while the rhythmic clang of the eggs being beaten in copper bowls provides the background music in the dining room.

SERVES 1

2 eggs, separated
Salt and pepper
30 g (1 oz) butter

1 Break the eggs into a large bowl and season generously with salt and pepper. Using a large balloon whisk or an electric mixer, beat the eggs until they are foamy and tripled in volume. Preheat the grill to hot (unless you are cooking over an open fire, where the flames licking up will cook the top of the omelette).

2 Heat the butter in a well seasoned omelette pan or small, heavy frying pan with a heatproof handle over medium heat, until it sizzles.

3 Pour the eggs into the pan and stir once gently with a fork. Continue cooking, without stirring, until the omelette is browned on the bottom and puffed, about 2 minutes. Transfer to the grill and grill just until the top is set but not dry. Fold the omelette in half and slide on to a warm plate.

Visitors flock to the village nestled at the base of the abbey, some in search of the special omelette at La Mère Poulard.

There must be as many different apple tarts as there are local varieties of apples in Normandy. Apples are enjoyed in almost every conceivable way and the drinks made from them, Calvados and cider, are synonymous with the region.

At the Apple House, *La Maison de la Pomme*, in Sainte-Opportune-la-Mare, fritters are on offer at the apple market held on the first Sunday of the month from November to Easter. Cooked on the spot, they are wonderful washed down with one of the local sparkling ciders, available for tasting here. Home-made apple tarts are for sale, as well as

Fruit Desserts and Confections

crates of apples grown on nearby farms. Inside the thatch-roofed former schoolhouse is information on apples and their cultivation and on cider-making.

The Apple House has a conservation orchard, one of several in Normandy, with 50 apple varieties under cultivation. Since the 1930s, a real crusade for the improvement of cider has prompted systematic study of the apple varieties used for cider-making, as well as technological advances in the process. Separate AOC designations for cider and Calvados made in certain areas

in Normandy acknowledge their special qualities. No less than six gastronomic societies promote the interests of cider, Calvados and Pommeau, with the *Confrérie des Chevaliers du Trou Normand* counting over 4000 members.

The cider made in Normandy is a blend of the juices of very tart cider apples and sweeter apples – even varietal cider has small additions. The apples, picked or shaken from the branches after they have already started to fall, are left to mature in lofts until they are soft; then they are washed and crushed. The juice is pressed from the crushed apple pulp and allowed to stand in vats until impurities rise to the top. The clear liquid at the bottom is drained off and fermented in barrels. Some cider is fermented in the bottle,

known as *cidre bouché*, a premium cider. Many farmers who make cider offer tastings, as do cider factories. Calvados is distilled from cider just as brandy is from wine, by boiling until the alcohol is released in vapours which are captured and liquified. The liquid may be re-distilled to concentrate and further purify it before maturation or put directly into oak barrels to age, for up to six years or more. Calvados is made in all the *départements* in Normandy, but the double-distilled Calvados has a special AOC, *Calvados du Pays d'Auge*. Traditionally, Calvados was poured into morning coffee,

served after dinner, and in the middle of a heavy meal the *trou normand*, a shot of Calvados, now usually in the form of sorbet, was taken to aid digestion.

Pommeau, an *apéritif* made from the juice of cider apples combined with Calvados and aged in wood, is enjoying renewed popularity. Formerly a home brew shared informally, it now appears in fine restaurants.

Pear cider, *poiré*, is a speciality of the area around Domfront in the Orne, and the local Calvados is often distilled from a mixture of pear and apple ciders. Calvados, cider and other apple alcohols of the region are used extensively in the cooking of Normandy. In making desserts, sweet cider is usually preferable and may also be served to accompany them.

Bénédictine must be included among the alcohols of Normandy, although it does not come from fruit, but derives

An ancient building near St. Julien sur Calonne offers a view of a Calvados maturing barrel and bottling machine.

its unique flavour from a blend of 27 herbs and spices. Made in Fécamp, once an entry point for spices in Normandy, when Dieppe was the centre for ivory carving on the "ivory and spice" route, it is a distillation based on the fifteenth-century recipe of a Benedictine monk.

Apples may be the fruit that Normandy is known for, but they are certainly not the only one. In addition to pears, which are prolific, berry farms dot the Seine valley. In summer, the markets display a rainbow-hued selection of strawberries, raspberries, blackberries and gooseberries. The energetic can even go to the source and pick their own. Vernon, near Monet's home, is the cherry capital of Normandy. In spring, the blossoms garland the boughs; in June the trees are bright with fruit and the cherry fair draws crowds to this attractive town.

The combination of Normandy's dairy products with the superb fruit grown here produces a tempting array of traditional desserts, from a simple topping of tangy *crème fraîche* on fresh berries to a warm apple custard tart to the creamy rice pudding still found in country kitchens.

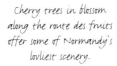

Cherry trees in blossom along the route des fruits offer some of Normandy's loveliest scenery.

Tarte aux Pommes Flambée au Calvados

CALVADOS APPLE TART

*This simple tart, a speciality of Calvados, really glorifies
the apple. The flavour of the fruit is the focus and the locally produced
apple brandy intensifies it.*

SERVES 6

1 kg (2 lb) medium dessert apples	FOR THE BUTTER SHORTCRUST PASTRY
2 tablespoons fresh lemon juice	210 g (7 oz) plain flour
60 g (2 oz) caster sugar	¼ teaspoon salt
75 g (2½ oz) butter	120 g (4 oz) cold butter, cut in pieces
3 tablespoons Calvados	1 egg yolk
Crème fraîche, to serve	2–3 tablespoons cold water

1 For the pastry, sift the flour and salt into a bowl. Add the butter and rub in until the mixture resembles coarse crumbs. Beat the egg yolk with 2 tablespoons of the water and sprinkle over the dough. Continue working the dough lightly, adding more water if needed, until it holds together and does not stick to your fingers. Form into a disc, wrap tightly and chill for at least 30 minutes.

2 Combine the apple slices with the lemon juice and all but a tablespoon of the sugar. Melt the butter in a large, heavy frying-pan over medium heat and add the apple mixture. Cook, stirring frequently, until the apples just start to colour, about 10 minutes. Let the apples cool in the pan off the heat.

3 Preheat the oven to 190°C/375°F/Gas Mark 5. On a lightly floured surface, roll the dough into a circle about 30 cm (12 inches) in diameter. Trim the edge if uneven. Roll the pastry around the rolling pin and transfer it to a lightly greased baking sheet, unrolling it over the baking sheet.

4 Place the apples on the pastry, leaving a 3.5 cm (1½-inch) border all around. Turn up the border and gather it around the apples, enclosing the outer apples. Bake for 20 minutes.

5 Heat the Calvados in a small saucepan and set it alight. Pour the flaming Calvados over the tart and sprinkle with the remaining sugar. Continue baking for about 15 minutes more, or until the pastry is crisp and the apples well browned. Serve warm, with crème fraîche.

Cook's Notes

The freeform shape gives the tart a rustic country look. If you prefer a more formal presentation, use the pastry to line a 20–23 cm (8–9 inch), loose-bottomed tart tin.

Apple brandy with the special AOC classification, Calvados du Pays d'Auge, is distilled twice before it is aged in wooden casks like these.

Douillons

APPLES IN PUFF PASTRY

These apple pastries appear in pastry shops everywhere in Normandy, as well as similar, pastry-enclosed apple confections, bourdalots. *Serve the pastries warm, with sweetened crème fraîche.*

SERVES 4

60 g (2 oz) ground almonds
4 tablespoons caster sugar
1 egg, separated
240 ml (8 fl oz) crème fraîche
360 g (12 oz) puff pastry
4 medium tart-sweet apples,
peeled and cored

1 egg, beaten with
1 teaspoon water, to glaze
3 tablespoons Pommeau
or Calvados
2 teaspoons icing sugar,
or to taste

Attractive pastry shops abound, offering a tempting selection of sweets — both regional specialities and classic creations.

1 In a small bowl, stir together the ground almonds, a tablespoon of the sugar, the egg yolk and 2 tablespoons of the crème fraîche, until well mixed.

2 Roll the pastry dough into a large square shape about 3 mm (⅛ inch) thick. Trim the edges to form a square 25 cm (10 inches) on each side and cut into quarters to form four 12.5 cm (5-inch) squares.

3 Sprinkle the apples with the remaining sugar. Set an apple in the centre of each pastry square. Spoon the almond mixture into the apples, dividing it evenly. Lightly beat the egg white and brush the edges of the pastry squares with it. Bring the corners together to form a parcel around the apple, pinching the edges together to enclose it completely. Cut leaf shapes from the pastry scraps and stick them on with egg white, to decorate. Refrigerate for an hour. Preheat the oven to 190°C/375°F/Gas Mark 5.

4 Brush the pastries with the egg glaze and bake for 30–40 minutes, or until they are deep golden brown. Leave to cool on a rack, for at least 10 minutes.

5 Whisk the remaining crème fraîche with the Pommeau or Calvados and add icing sugar to taste. Serve the pastries warm, with the flavoured cream.

Tarte Normande aux Pommes

APPLE CUSTARD TART

*There seems to be an infinite variety of apple tarts in Normandy – almost as many
as there are varieties of apples. In this tart, a creamy custard balances any
sharpness in the apples.*

SERVES 6

360 g (12 oz) butter
shortcrust pastry
(see page 78)
1 egg white, beaten
until frothy
500 g (1 lb) dessert apples,
peeled, cored and very
thinly sliced

60 g (2 oz) caster sugar
Grated zest of ½ lemon
Freshly grated nutmeg or
ground cinnamon
2 eggs
240 ml (8 fl oz) double or
whipping cream
¼ teaspoon vanilla essence

1 Preheat the oven to 200°C/400°F/Gas Mark 6.

2 Roll out the pastry dough to a thickness of about 6 mm
(¼ inch) and line a 23 cm (9-inch) tart tin. Lightly prick the
bottom of the pastry case and line it with foil. Fill the foil
with dried beans or baking weights to make a thick layer.
Bake for 15 minutes, until the edge is slightly dry and set.
Remove the foil and beans, brush the inside of the pastry
case thinly with egg white and continue baking for 5
minutes. Remove to a wire rack. Reduce the oven
temperature to 180°C/350°F/Gas Mark 4.

3 Toss the apple slices with half the sugar, the lemon
zest and a pinch of nutmeg or cinnamon. Arrange them in
the pastry case, overlapping, in concentric circles.

4 Whisk the eggs and remaining sugar until well combined and whisk in the cream and vanilla essence.
Carefully pour the custard mixture over the apples and
bake for 45–50 minutes, until the top is a rich gold colour
and a knife inserted in the custard comes out clean. Serve
warm or at room temperature.

Charlotte aux Pommes

APPLE CHARLOTTE

The annual contest for the prize apple charlotte is one of many gastronomic competitions held all over Normandy. The apple charlottes entered for competition are usually cold. This recipe is for the traditional hot apple charlotte.

SERVES 6

1.2 kg (2½ lb) dessert apples
2 tablespoons water
1 cinnamon stick
120 g (4 oz) caster sugar

1 firm-textured brioche loaf
(preferably stale), about
240 g (8 oz)
75 g (2½ oz) butter, melted

1 Cut the apples, unpeeled, into quarters and put them in a large, heavy saucepan, with the water and cinnamon stick. Cover and cook over medium-low heat until very soft, about 20 minutes, stirring frequently. Work the apples through a food mill and return the purée to the saucepan. Add the sugar and continue cooking, uncovered, for about 10 minutes more, stirring almost constantly, until the apple purée is very thick. (There should be about 750 ml/1¼ pints.)

2 Preheat the oven to 200°C/400°F/Gas Mark 6. Trim the crusts from the brioche and slice it thinly. Brush the slices with melted butter on one side. Cut two slices into triangles and use as many as necessary to cover the bottom of a 1.5-litre (2¼-pint) charlotte mould or soufflé dish, placing them buttered-side down and fitting them tightly. Cut rectangular pieces of brioche the same height as the mould and place them buttered-side against the mould, without any spaces between.

3 Pour the apple purée into the mould. Cover the top with brioche, buttered-side up, cut as necessary to fit. Bake for 20 minutes, reduce the heat to 180°C/350°F/Gas Mark 4 and continue baking for about 25 minutes more, until well browned and firm. Let stand for 15 minutes before unmoulding on to a serving plate.

Beignets des Pommes

APPLE FRITTERS

These crispy fritters are traditional regional fare in all parts of Normandy. They are best coated and cooked just before eating, but the apples can be prepared ahead and the batter, too, except for whisking and folding in the egg whites.

SERVES 4

100 g (3½ oz) self-raising flour
Pinch of salt
3 tablespoons icing sugar,
plus more for dusting
2 eggs, separated
150 ml (¼ pint) sparkling
sweet or dry cider

15 g (½ oz) butter, melted
4 medium eating apples
Lemon juice
1 tablespoon caster sugar
Oil for deep-frying

1 Sift the flour, salt and icing sugar into a medium bowl and make a well in the centre. Whisk together the egg yolks and cider and slowly pour them into the well, whisking constantly and gradually bringing in the flour, until the batter is smooth and will fall from the whisk in a ribbon. Whisk in the melted butter and let the batter stand for about an hour.

2 Peel and core the apples. Slice into rings about 6 mm (¼ inch) thick and sprinkle with lemon juice.

3 Whisk the egg whites until soft peaks form. Sprinkle on the caster sugar and continue beating just until firm. Fold the egg whites into the batter.

4 Heat the oil in a deep-fryer to a temperature of 190°C/375°F (or until a cube of bread browns in 40 seconds). Pat the apple rings dry. Using a fork, dip the apples into the batter, a few at a time, and fry until golden and puffed on both sides, turning once. Drain on kitchen paper and dust with icing sugar for serving.

Some of the many varieties of Normandy apples are on display.

Tarte aux Cerises et au Fromage Blanc

CHERRY CHEESE FLAN

The Seine valley is perfect for fruit cultivation, and the route des fruits will lead you through some lovely countryside. The combination of cherries with the rich, creamy fresh cheese from this area is a regional classic.

SERVES 6

360 g (12 oz) cherries, stoned
2 tablespoons Calvados
or kirsch
2 eggs
60 g (2 oz) caster sugar
210 g (7 oz) fromage blanc
or soft cheese, unsalted

if possible, at room
temperature
5 tablespoons crème fraîche
or double cream
½ teaspoon vanilla essence

1 Put the cherries in a bowl with the Calvados or kirsch and leave to stand for at least 30 minutes.

2 Preheat the oven to 190°C/375°F/Gas Mark 5. Lightly butter a 23 cm (9-inch) ceramic tart mould.

3 Using an electric mixer, beat together the eggs and sugar until thick and lighter in colour. Add the cheese, cream and vanilla, and continue beating until smooth and well blended.

4 Drain the cherries and add the liquid to the cheese mixture, stirring to combine. Arrange the cherries in the mould and pour over the cheese mixture.

5 Bake for 30–35 minutes, or until golden and set. Serve warm or at room temperature.

Cherry trees laden with fruit are a beautiful sight in summer.

Tarte aux Poires Frangipane

PEAR AND ALMOND-CREAM TART

This tart can be found in almost every good pâtisserie in Normandy. Of course, it can also be made with apples and flavoured with a little Calvados!

SERVES 6

360 g (12 oz) butter
shortcrust pastry (page 78)
1 egg white, lightly beaten
100 g (3½ oz) ground almonds
60 g (2 oz) caster sugar
75 g (2½ oz) butter
1 egg

1 egg yolk
1 tablespoon crème fraîche
or double cream
4 tablespoons pear liqueur
4 firm, ripe, small pears
3 tablespoons runny honey

1 Preheat the oven to 200°C/400°F/Gas Mark 6. Roll out the pastry dough to a thickness of about 6 mm (¼ inch) and line a 23 cm (9-inch) tart tin. Lightly prick the bottom of the pastry case and line with foil. Fill the foil with dried beans or baking weights to make a thick layer. Bake for 15 minutes, until the edge is slightly dry and set. Remove the foil and beans, brush the inside of the pastry case thinly with egg white and continue baking for 5 minutes. Remove to a wire rack. Reduce the oven temperature to 180°C/350°F/Gas Mark 4.

2 Meanwhile, mix the ground almonds, sugar and butter in a food processor or with an electric mixer until combined. Add the butter and mix until creamy; then mix in the egg, egg yolk, cream and 2 tablespoons of the liqueur. Pour the almond filling into the tart shell.

3 Peel, core and halve the pears. Put the pear halves cut-side down and slice them thinly crossways, keeping the slices together. Slide a palette knife under each pear half and press it on top to fan out the slices. Transfer the pear halves to the tart shell, placing the fruit on the filling like the spokes of a wheel. Fill in gaps around the edge with any leftover pear. Bake for 35–40 minutes, until lightly browned. Transfer to a rack to cool.

4 In a small saucepan, melt the honey with the remaining liqueur over low heat and brush over the tart.

Soufflé Domfrontais

PEAR SOUFFLÉ

Pears are used to make cider, called poiré *or perry. The fruit is pressed right after picking, not left to mature like cider apples, and the liquid is pale and clear. Sadly, this speciality of Domfront in the Orne is not widely exported.*

SERVES 4

500 ml (16 fl oz) pear cider or medium-sweet apple cider
120 g (4 oz) caster sugar
2 large pears, peeled, cored and halved
1 vanilla pod, split
90 ml (3 fl oz) whipping cream

2 tablespoons plain flour
2 tablespoons pear liqueur or Calvados
3 eggs, at room temperature, separated
1 egg white, at room temperature
Pinch of cream of tartar

1 Put the cider in a small saucepan (preferably stainless steel) large enough to hold the pears in one layer. Set aside 30 g (1 oz) of the sugar and add the remainder to the cider, stirring to dissolve. Add the pear halves and vanilla pod, topping up with more cider if the fruit is not covered. Bring to the boil, reduce the heat to low and simmer until tender, about 15 minutes. Remove the pears and reduce the syrup to 120 ml (4 fl oz). Stir in the cream.

2 Preheat the oven to 190°C/375°F/Gas Mark 5. Lightly butter a 30 cm (12-inch) oval gratin dish or a 1.5-litre (2¼-pint) shallow baking dish.

3 Sift the flour into a heavy saucepan and slowly add the cider and cream mixture, whisking constantly until completely smooth. Set the pan over a medium heat and bring to the boil, stirring constantly. Add the liqueur and boil for 10 seconds, stirring. Remove from the heat and beat in the egg yolks, one at a time.

4 Put the four egg whites and cream of tartar in a large bowl. Using an electric mixer, beat slowly until the mixture becomes frothy. Increase the speed gradually to moderately high and beat until soft peaks form. Sprinkle over the remaining sugar and continue beating until firm peaks form.

5 Stir a spoonful of beaten egg whites into the soufflé mixture, to lighten it. Pour the mixture over the whites and, using a large rubber spatula or metal spoon, quickly and lightly fold until they are just combined.

6 Arrange the pears in the dish, cut-side down. Spoon the soufflé mixture into the dish, mounding it over the pears. Bake for 18–20 minutes, until puffed and golden brown; serve immediately.

Truffes au Chocolat Aromatisées au Bénédictine

CHOCOLATE TRUFFLES WITH BENEDICTINE

Simone Beck, whose grandfather founded the Benedictine distillery in Fécamp, shared this essentially simple chocolate truffle recipe with me. Use only the best quality chocolate.

MAKES ABOUT 60 TRUFFLES

500 g (1 lb) bittersweet chocolate, chopped
4 tablespoons water
210 g (7 oz) cold unsalted butter, cut in pieces

100 ml (3½ fl oz) Benedictine liqueur
5–6 tablespoons unsweetened cocoa powder

1 Put the chocolate in a heatproof bowl or the top of a double-boiler, add the water and set over barely simmering water (do not allow the water underneath to touch the bowl or to boil). Let stand for 3–5 minutes, then stir frequently until melted and smooth.

2 Remove the bowl from the heat and beat in the butter, a few pieces at a time, until the mixture is smooth. Stir in the liqueur and let stand until completely cool, or refrigerate for about 30 minutes until the mixture is just beginning to set.

3 Drop the mixture by teaspoonfuls on to a baking sheet lined with greaseproof paper. Refrigerate for 20–30 minutes, until firm.

4 Sift the cocoa powder into a shallow dish. One at a time, roll the truffles in cocoa until well coated and transfer to paper cases.

Riz au Lait aux Pommes Pochées

SLOW-COOKED RICE PUDDING WITH POACHED APPLES

*Known by various regional names, this creamy rice pudding
typifies Norman home cooking. The addition of poached apples
makes a lighter dessert.*

SERVES 4

1.75 litres (3 pints) milk
150 g (5 oz) brown sugar
150 g (5 oz) short-grain
or pudding rice
Pinch of salt
Pinch of nutmeg

2 apples, peeled, cored
and halved
300 ml (½ pint) sweet cider
2–3 tablespoons caster sugar
Cinnamon stick

1 Preheat the oven to 150°C/300°F/Gas Mark 2. Heat the milk in a large saucepan over medium-high heat, until bubbles appear around the edge. Reduce the heat to low and stir in the sugar.

2 Rinse the rice in a sieve. Put the rice, salt and nutmeg in a deep earthenware casserole or baking dish, about 2½-litre (4-pint) capacity. Slowly pour over the milk mixture, stirring thoroughly to prevent the rice forming lumps, and put in the oven. Stir twice during the first hour, then allow the pudding to form a crust and continue baking until the crust is deep golden brown, about 3 hours in all.

3 Meanwhile, put the apples in a small saucepan (preferably stainless steel) with the cider, sugar and cinnamon stick. Bring to the boil, reduce the heat to low and simmer until just tender, 15–20 minutes. Serve the apples warm or at room temperature, with the rice pudding.

Local farms' milk gives this dessert its smooth, creamy texture.

Menu planner

Norman food celebrates the regional products. A first course is customary, followed by meat, poultry or fish. Family meals often conclude with cheese and salad or fresh fruit, and desserts are more likely at weekends or in restaurants. Known for its dairy products, the food in Normany is rich by most people's standards. Feel free to substitute leaner choices. These menus generally serve 4.

As Normandy is not a wine-producing region, the local cider is often served with meals. Otherwise, French wines suitable to each course would be served.

LUNCH BY THE QUAY

Fresh Oysters – or
Oeufs en cocotte Marie Herel 71
Baked eggs with Camembert cheese

Marmite Dieppoise 20
Normandy seafood stew

Douillons 80
Apples in puff pastry

COASTAL DINNER

Palourdes à la persillade 21
Clams with garlic and parsley butter

Barbue à l'oseille 29
Brill with sorrel sauce

Selection of Normandy cheeses

Truffes au chocolat aromatisées au Bénédictine 88
Chocolate truffles with Benedictine

BISTRO DINNER

Soufflé au Livarot 64
Livarot cheese soufflé

Suprême de volaille au cresson 41
Chicken breasts with watercress sauce

Carottes et échalotes étuvées au beurre 55
Glazed carrots and shallots

Beignets des pommes 83
Apple fritters

SUNDAY SUPPER

Salade de betteraves au vinaigrette de noisette 59
Beetroot salad with hazelnut vinaigrette

Gratin des coquillages 22
Shellfish gratin

Tarte aux pommes flambée au Calvados 78
Calvados apple tart

SIMPLE FAMILY DINNER

Salade Cauchoise 58
Normandy potato salad

Truite meunière aux noisettes 28
Trout with hazelnuts

Riz au lait aux pommes pochées 89
Slow-cooked rice pudding with poached apples

FARMHOUSE FARE

Moules au cidre et à la crème 23
Mussels steamed in cider with cream

Pintade au chou à la Normande 43
Guinea fowl with cabbage and apples

Tarte aux poires frangipane 85
Pear and almond-cream tart

SUMMER SOLSTICE BONFIRE DINNER

Omelette Mère Poulard 73
Soufflé-omelette Mère Poulard

Navarin d'agneau de pré-salé 36
Lamb stew with spring vegetables

Tarte au cerises et au fromage blanc 84
Cherry cheese flan

AUTUMN DINNER

Brioches aux champignons sauvages 52
Wild mushrooms in brioches

Pavé de chevreuil au Camembert 46
Venison steak with Camembert cheese sauce

Blettes à la crème 56
Chard with cream

Soufflé Domfrontais 86
Pear soufflé

FIRESIDE DINNER

Tartelettes au Neufchâtel 65
Neufchâtel and spinach tartlets

Cailles au cidre et au vinaigre 45
Quails with onions, cider and cider vinegar

Gratin de poireaux et de pommes de terre 57
Leek and potato gratin

Charlotte aux pommes 82
Apple charlotte

Index

Credits

Quarto Publishing would like to thank the following for permission to reproduce copyright material:

Key: a – above; b – below

French Picture Library pp 2 & 41, Denis Hughes-Gilbey pp 7 & 8, Pictor p 9, Jeff Goodman/Travel Ink p 10, Sopexa (UK) Ltd p 13, Stefano Caporali p 14, Alain Choisnet/Image Bank p 17 a, French Picture Library pp 17 b & 18, Abbie Enock/Travel Ink p 23, PictureBank p 24, French Picture Library p 27, Pictor p 28, French Picture Library p 31, Ray Mitchell/Travel Ink p 32, Derek Bermin/Image Bank p 33, Mary Jacobsen/Ace p 34, Denis Hughes-Gilbey p 37, French Picture Library p 38, Sopexa (UK) Ltd pp 42 & 45, Mauritius/Ace p 46, Christel Rosenfeld/Image Bank p 49, French Picture Library p 50, R. Nuettgens/Image p 51, French Picture Library p 52, Bullaty/Lomeo/Image Bank p 55, Ian Cook p 56, Pictor 59, David W. Hamilton/Image Bank p 61, Denis Hughes-Gilbey p 62, Stockphotos/Image Bank p 64, J. Allan Cash p 67, Richard Walker/Ace p 70, J. Allan Cash p 67, J. Allan Cash p 73, Denish Hughes-Gilbey p 75, Stuart Boreham/Cephas p 76, Benelux Press/Ace p 77, Ian Cook p 79, John Searle/Ace p 80, David W. Hamilton/Image Bank p 83, Denis Hughes-Gilbey p 84, David W. Hamilton/Image Bank p 89.

While every effort has been made to acknowledge all copyright holders, we apologize
if any omissions have been made.